Level Best

Additional Titles from Chardon Press

JB JOSSEY-BASS

Level Best

HOW SMALL AND GRASSROOTS NONPROFITS CAN TACKLE EVALUATION AND TALK RESULTS

Marcia Festen
Marianne Philbin

John Wiley & Sons, Inc.

Published by Jossey-Bass
A Wiley Imprint
989 Market Street, San Francisco, CA 94103-1741   www.josseybass.com

The materials that appear in this book (except those for which reprint permission must be obtained from the primary sources) may be reproduced for educational/training activities. We do, however, require that the following statement appear on all reproductions:

Level Best: How Small and Grassroots Nonprofits Can Tackle Evaluation and Talk Results, by Marcia Festen and Marianne Philbin.

Copyright © 2007 by John Wiley & Sons, Inc.

This free permission is limited to the reproduction of material for educational/training events. Systematic or large-scale reproduction or distribution (more than one hundred copies per year)—or inclusion of items in publications for sale—may be done only with prior written permission. Also, reproduction on computer disk or by any other electronic means requires prior written permission. Requests to the Publisher for permission should be addressed to the Permissions Department, John Wiley & Sons, Inc., 111 River Street, Hoboken, NJ 07030, 201-748-6011, fax 201-748-6008, or online at http://www.wiley.com/go/permissions.

Readers should be aware that Internet Web sites offered as citations and/or sources for further information may have changed or disappeared between the time this was written and when it is read.

Jossey-Bass books and products are available through most bookstores. To contact Jossey-Bass directly call our Customer Care Department within the U.S. at 800-956-7739, outside the U.S. at 317-572-3986, or fax 317-572-4002.

Jossey-Bass also publishes its books in a variety of electronic formats. Some content that appears in print may not be available in electronic books.

Library of Congress Cataloging-in-Publication Data

Festen, Marcia, date.
  Level best: how small and grassroots nonprofits can tackle
evaluation and talk results/Marcia Festen, Marianne Philbin.
      p. cm.
  Includes bibliographical references and index.
    ISBN-13: 978-0-7879-7906-5 (pbk.)
    ISBN-10: 0-7879-7906-6 (pbk.)
  1. Nonprofit organizations—Evaluation. 2. Nonprofit
organizations—Management. I. Philbin, Marianne. II. Title.
    HD62.6.F475 2007
    658.4'013—dc22
                                    2006023713

FIRST EDITION
PB Printing   10 9 8 7 6 5 4 3 2 1

THE CHARDON PRESS SERIES

Fundamental social change happens when people come together to organize, advo-
cate, and create solutions to injustice. Chardon Press recognizes that communities
working for social justice need tools to create and sustain healthy organizations. In
an effort to support these organizations, Chardon Press produces materials on fundraising, community organizing, and organizational development. These resources
are specifically designed to meet the needs of grassroots nonprofits—organizations
that face the unique challenge of promoting change with limited staff, funding, and
other resources. We at Chardon Press have adapted traditional techniques to the cir-
cumstances of grassroots nonprofits. Chardon Press and Jossey-Bass hope these
works help people committed to social justice to build mission-driven organizations
that are strong, financially secure, and effective.

Kim Klein, Series Editor

CONTENTS

To Willa and Genevieve, Ruby and Ella

FIGURE, TABLES, WORKSHEETS, EXHIBITS, AGENDAS

FIGURE

TABLES

WORKSHEETS

EXHIBITS

AGENDAS

INTRODUCTION

Everything that can be counted does not necessarily count,
and everything that counts cannot necessarily be counted.

Albert Einstein

*T*he expression "Do your level best" means "Make your very best
  effort." As we talked with nonprofit leaders about this book, we
began to think of "level best" as the level to which all nonprofits aspire.
Solid program evaluation can help nonprofits achieve that level of
performance.

The expression originated during the California gold rush of the 1840s, when
people panning for gold would shake the sand and gravel from the riverbed until
it was level, the better to spot the fragments of gold. This book will help you become more capable and confident about evaluation so that you can make the
"gold" in your work stand out.

Level Best is intended for new and established grassroots and smaller nonprofit
organizations that seek better measures to document and share results in ways that
are practical, efficient, and meaningful. Our goal is to help demystify evaluation and
to offer practical strategies that enable more confident decision making, sound program and organizational planning, and increased accountability and credibility.

A recent study by the National Committee for Responsive Philanthropy (Bothwell, 2000) of foundation funding to grassroots organizations found that foundations tend to fund fewer grassroots organizations than other types of nonprofit organizations, in part because "foundations require accountability, measurement and documentation beyond what grassroots organizations can do." The study notes that "grassroots organizations need to develop public identities, use the media, construct more attractive funding packets, and last but not least, *document what they've done and tell their stories better.*"

Solid evaluation is the first step toward increasing organizational effectiveness and, in turn, successfully marketing and documenting your work. *Level Best* offers solutions to evaluation challenges at each stage of the process, taking readers through the steps needed to: design or improve an evaluation process; determine what to measure and why; track results; and put findings to use in a way that helps organizations become stronger and better at what they do.

Each chapter of this book addresses one of the five stages in our evaluation framework: Planning, Asking, Tracking, Learning, Using. The system is designed with volunteer leadership in mind and with a "do-it-yourself" spirit. In this book, we also introduce a concept we're calling "rolling evaluation," which suggests a way for smaller nonprofits to take on evaluation and commit to it year-by-year without overloading themselves.

The approach that we are introducing in this book—rolling evaluation—allows you to ask and answer a limited number of questions each year, build on what you learn year by year, and continually add depth and detail to the portrait you are painting of your organization and its work. If your organization has the capacity to explore more than one or two questions per year or to evaluate more than one program or priority, that's terrific, and the steps recommended here can still be applied.

As we emphasize throughout the book, our approach to evaluation begins with the premise that evaluation should not be considered an "add-on" or an occasional special project but should be seen as part and parcel of your ongoing work to fulfill your mission, plan your programs, and raise money.

HOW TO USE THIS BOOK

We intend for this guide to be useful to in-house staff that may be conducting an evaluation, the consultants who might be working with you, and the board members or volunteer leaders (or both) who need to understand evaluation better in order to plan and oversee it.

We also intend for this book to make evaluation as easy as possible and to provide you with what you need to know—without forcing you to plow through volumes of text or countless case studies. We lay out some basic principles that will help you plan for a realistic and manageable evaluation process, and we provide step-by-step guidance in the form of ready-made meeting agendas and other materials. We recommend that you read through the book at least one time before pulling specific forms or exercises to use, so that you have a clear sense of where you're ultimately going.

We suggest that you use this book to *construct what you are going to do from this day forward rather than analyze what you did in the past.* If you didn't build strategies for evaluation into your work plan last year—or the year before that—is it really feasible for you to attempt to evaluate what you did *during* that time? It is much more difficult to apply evaluation techniques after the fact than it is to gather what you need as you go forward. Evaluating years or decades of past work can be done, but if you have a limited budget and if you have a choice, concentrate your resources on the present, taking into consideration what you know about your past. The work the organization is doing now, after all, will need to be understood and reshaped or re-funded twelve months from now.

In easy-to-follow steps that take your operating realities into consideration, *Level Best* gives you the tools to develop your evaluation plan, gather your data, and use the lessons you learn to strengthen your organization, as well as your ability to make the case for continued support.

INSTRUCTION WITH SAMPLES AND EXAMPLES

Drawing on our own experience and the expertise of evaluation professionals and nonprofit managers, we've included samples of forms, checklists, and other materials that small and grassroots organizations have found useful. Especially helpful, we believe, will be the sample meeting agendas included at the end of each chapter. You can use them as is or adapt them as needed, as you and your committee move through your evaluation cycle.

The sample meeting agendas are based on the assumption that board or volunteer leaders will be playing a role in supporting or overseeing your evaluation process. They are designed to help you and your volunteers move through the process from start to finish. They can be combined or separated, and adapted for use as part of board, staff, or evaluation committee meetings, depending on your needs and structure.

Throughout *Level Best* we intersperse "examples" from four fictitious organizations that represent a composite of real nonprofits' experiences with evaluation. These organizations are as follows:

- Artists and Musicians for Literacy. Founded by artists to promote wider community investment in literacy programs, this organization presents concerts, exhibits, and readings to the general public in order to raise awareness and encourage community involvement in literacy efforts.

- Democracy Begins Here. A national organization with local parent group affiliates in communities around the country, the group works on school reform in public school systems by engaging parents in their children's education process.

- West Coast Network of Global Givers. This is a network of individuals who give money to international causes and work to increase philanthropic giving globally.

- East Morgan Neighborhood Network. This is a coalition of community residents working to create better schools, jobs, affordable housing, sustainable land use, neighborhood safety, and youth and senior-citizen activities.

Level Best

Understanding Evaluation

T his chapter summarizes the context in which today's nonprofits are working, providing background that is important to understand as you undertake evaluation. In part, it answers the question, Why evaluate? A first step for many smaller organizations involves "adjusting" their internal mind-set and thinking about evaluation in a new way.

To some extent, all nonprofits operate on instinct. Necessity may be the mother of invention, as the old saying goes, but in the nonprofit world instinct is often the mother of *action.* Our instincts lead us to potential board members, to form strategic alliances, and to develop new and original ideas for special events or for programs we believe we uniquely can develop. The longer nonprofit leaders are in the field, the more their instincts are honed, and the better able they are to identify a real prospect for a contribution, an alliance that could be mutually beneficial, or a strategy that could offer a new solution. Nonprofit staffs routinely find themselves sharing their instincts as they identify community needs and brainstorm about what can be done to address them.

In the nonprofit sector, we pride ourselves on our instincts, because for nonprofits, instinct and good judgment are necessary for survival. We have little time and little money. We have to get the job done, and do it right.

In recent years, however, nonprofits have been challenged to defend their instincts and explain their assumptions—to assess the impact of their work, both for their own learning and in order to "prove" that what they *think* is good actually *is* good, that what they claim as results are indeed results.

Instinct is important, but instinct alone is not enough. Donors increasingly want specifics in order to continue funding (and because their own reputations are at stake); legislators want greater oversight from boards; media want facts that shore up assumptions; program participants want and deserve accountability, and constituents and other partners want information that clearly shows an organization's specific contributions to the community.

This increased interest in nonprofit results and accountability has many sources, ranging from the explosion of information available via the Internet to desire by government agencies for more oversight of the nonprofit sector. Corporate scandals at companies like Enron and Arthur Andersen led Congress to pass legislation related to "corporate accountability" in 2002; the Senate Finance Committee began to discuss the need to more closely regulate the nonprofit sector as well.

Interest in greater accountability has also come from within the sector. One nonprofit leadership forum, Independent Sector, for example, recently issued more than one hundred recommendations intended to strengthen the ability of the nation's 1.3 million charities and foundations to serve as "responsible stewards of the public's generosity."

"Foundation and nonprofit organization accountability" emerged as an area of major concern in research conducted by the Center for Nonprofit and Philanthropic Leadership at Rutgers University in 2004 (Capek, 2004). Survey respondents, when asked to identify critical issues and trends facing the nonprofit sector, said that both foundations and nonprofits were "missing opportunities for crucial rethinking as to how to do their best work" (p. 2). Many described foundations and nonprofits as prone to working in isolation and as lacking sufficient opportunities for straight talk and feedback.

With calls for tougher standards coming from many directions, the nonprofit sector is expected to face sweeping changes over the next several years in legal oversight and regulation of activities. Much of the regulation is likely to focus on how nonprofits spend and manage their money and how carefully boards of directors attend to their roles and responsibilities, including the oversight of programs.

What you learn through evaluation and how you apply it will communicate your commitment to accountability as well as how well your organization is working toward meeting its mission. No matter what changes or regulations are ultimately implemented at the state or federal level, evidence that evaluation is a priority will be one indicator of how well nonprofit organizations are attending to their core duties.

EVALUATION AS POWER INSTEAD OF PAIN

The term *evaluation* still connotes a test that can be passed or failed, a judgment issued at the end of a long stretch of independent, completed work. Nonprofit organizations need to begin thinking of evaluation differently—not as a pass-fail, right-wrong, good-bad hurdle but as part of a process that provides useful information that helps your organization learn more, plan better, and operate more efficiently. In addition to understanding the climate surrounding evaluation, it's important to examine (and possibly change!) the prevailing mind-set about evaluation within your own organization.

Seeing evaluation as a lot of added, new work, nonprofit managers often feel they have neither the time, the money, nor the staff trained to track, analyze, and produce evidence of organizational impact. Because nonprofits are overstretched in so many ways, the pressure to "do evaluation" can seem like just one more burden. After all, gathering data costs money. Tracking program participants or visitors costs money. Designing and administering surveys, holding focus groups, and maintaining records costs money. And it all takes time. As one executive director we spoke with put it,

> We share the same desire as our donors for concrete, definitive indications of the impact of our work. But most of us can only afford to do the most basic kinds of evaluation—the "counting," so to speak: how many people attended a meeting, how many sessions we offered, that kind of thing. Even the foundations with big bucks are discovering that "impact" is hard to define or prove—but they expect us to do it on a shoestring.

The pressure to conduct "an evaluation" hangs heavy over the heads of many smaller organizations. For grassroots organizations—small community-based and advocacy organizations—there can be additional challenges. Social change or social justice work is often difficult to quantify in traditional ways. Within social-change organizations, achievements might be measured in terms of relationships built, messages framed, or specific actions or campaigns undertaken in the community. But the results of these achievements on the larger stage can be hard to measure, and they take time to observe and understand.

If you look at evaluation as somehow separate from your other work—your "real work"—you will probably end up feeling overwhelmed and resentful. It is important to understand evaluation as *part* of your organization's real work—as a thread running through all that you do to achieve your mission, plan your program, and raise money.

Rather than seeing it as a burden, recognize its enormous value. Evaluation is of value because it gives nonprofits something they often feel that they lack: *control*. When you actively design and use evaluation as a tool to help you learn and grow, then evaluation becomes a resource and an opportunity for your organization to understand why it succeeds when it does succeed and to tell its story better. Understanding some of the factors behind the current emphasis on evaluation can help you anticipate the kinds of questions you might receive from your funders, board, colleagues, and constituents.

If you do not evaluate your programs yourself, you can bet that opinions will be formed about your work anyway, and decisions that affect you will be made based on those informal "evaluations." The philanthropic and nonprofit grapevines are active and often very powerful. Sadly, it is a common scenario for potential supporters to turn away from an organization because of "what they've heard" or because of a reputation hung over from a previous point in the organization's history. Evaluation offers the chance to replace impressions with facts.

Whether you know it or not, you and your programs are already being evaluated. Public opinion is the strongest evaluator a nonprofit organization faces and could be the only one if the organization does not have data to back up its claims of community value. Addressing public opinion is only one of many reasons an organization may want to evaluate its programs. Acquiring and continuing funding are other strong motivators.

The greatest reason to evaluate is to learn how you can provide the best service to your clients or constituents. Putting an evaluation program into place is the only way an organization can ascertain what is working well and what is cost-effective.

—Reid Zimmerman
Minnesota Council of Nonprofits

WHAT EVALUATION *IS* AND WHAT IT *IS NOT*

At its most basic, evaluation involves looking at your program during a specific period of time and asking, "Is what we're doing working? How do we know it's working?" and, often, "Under what conditions does it work best?"

Planning, Not Judging

The purpose of evaluation is to help you plan for next year, not to judge what you did in the past. One reason that the very idea of evaluation can seem so daunting to smaller groups is that evaluation implies making a judgment after something is over. It seems to suggest backtracking over territory that's already been covered and work that's already been done, with the hope of reconstructing what actually happened, and then determining whether it was worth the effort. Who wouldn't be exhausted at the mere thought of doing that?

Evaluation is not the "extra work" at the end of your project, the last-minute add-on that you do because everyone else is doing it. Rather, it is part of what you put in place *beforehand* to help you run your programs.

Evaluation is part of the continuum of planning. Evaluation encompasses a broad spectrum of activity but is essentially a systematic process of asking questions, then collecting and using the answers to

- Measure progress on priority issues and identify areas for improvement
- Set realistic goals by providing information for making and fine-tuning strategic program decisions
- Identify staff and volunteer training and technical-assistance needs

- Be accountable and credible to your constituents, your community, your partners, your funders, and yourself
- Motivate by providing documentation of your achievements
- Guide budget and resource allocations
- Generate support for programs and make the case for added resources
- Be an effective organization that works toward its mission

Evaluation is *not*

- A test or a punishment
- Something you design *only* as a means to promote your work or show off how brilliant you are.
- A scientific research project that requires control groups in order to prove or disprove a hypothesis
- Something you do every five years
- About expanding or about cutting your programs
- An occasional activity or a one-time event

Evaluating Versus Conducting Research

As you begin considering how you will tackle evaluation at your organization, it is important to acknowledge, with your evaluation team, whatever may be among your greatest sources of anxiety about the process (see Exhibit 1.1). Perhaps you are nervous about the time it might take away from other things; perhaps you are nervous about what you've heard from others or about evaluation seeming to require the skills of a professional researcher.

"I always tell my nonprofit clients that there is a distinction between research and evaluation," says evaluation consultant Susannah Quern Pratt, "and when I remind them of that, I generally see a huge look of relief cross their faces."

The pressure to evaluate and the misconceptions about what evaluation entails can lead many smaller groups to forego the effort altogether, assuming it requires specialized skills or rigor beyond their capacity. Although evaluation may draw from the techniques that researchers have pioneered, evaluation does not need to

Exhibit 1.1
Quick Exercise: Fears and Misperceptions

If you've never been involved in an evaluation or if you've had a bad experience with it in the past, you may have some anxiety going into the process. What are you afraid of? Address these concerns up-front by writing a brief memo that outlines for your board and staff why you are undertaking evaluation and what you believe you can accomplish with it, as well as what you consider to be beyond the evaluation's scope or intent (for example, what the evaluation won't tell you about your work).

COMMON FEARS AND MISPERCEPTIONS

Here are some of the usual barriers to getting evaluation under way:

- Our funders and supporters have false or elevated expectations of what an evaluation will tell us, and if it's too thin, it will end up making us look bad.
- Our goals could change in the course of the project we're evaluating, but the evaluation process will already be in play.
- We did not define our "desired outcomes" ahead of time; we are hoping an evaluation will show us the kind of outcomes we're getting.
- We really don't have the skills or resources to do it right.
- We don't have an evaluation expert working with us.
- Different audiences want different kinds of data—and different results.
- We're not sure we want to know what an evaluation might tell us.
- We feel under pressure to come up with the final, dramatic one-liner, as in "60 percent of our visitors did such-and-such. . . ."—but our work is really a story in progress.

HOW TO ADDRESS COMMON FEARS AND MISPERCEPTIONS

The best way to address all of the above is to articulate clearly the following:

- The goal *you* defined for your program, as opposed to something thrust upon you
- The steps you will undertake to conduct your evaluation
- The rationale for your choices
- The best response to the pressure you may feel to do an evaluation a certain way is to have a defensible plan of your own that makes sense for your organization.

be research, and small organizations can benefit enormously, as Pratt points out, by "shifting their thinking from 'prove' to 'improve.'"

Even in the best-case scenario, you are more likely to be able to gather *evidence* that what you are doing works rather than being able to provide *proof.*

Evaluating for the Wrong Reasons

Here are some *wrong reasons* for undertaking evaluation:

- You think you can raise money for it, and some of the dollars that you raise can be allocated to general operating costs.
- It's your anniversary.
- A funder requires it.
- You want support for a decision you intend to make anyway, regardless of what you learn in the course of evaluation.
- The board wants to get rid of a program or a staff person or the CEO.
- You want to prove to others how good your work is, rather than using evaluation to learn how to be better.

Creating Effective Organizations with Evaluation

Evaluation is a necessary ingredient to becoming an effective organization. Boards need the information that evaluation provides in order to make good decisions. Staff needs the information in order to plan and deliver effective programs. Funders need it in order to make a case for continuing their support. Evaluation provides nonprofit leaders with opportunities for new vision and new ways of solving problems, as well as with the confidence to learn and grow.

Think of evaluation as a tool designed to help you understand your organizational strengths and to throw some light on areas in need of improvement. It provides an opportunity for informed conversation and reflection; it engages your board and staff in the strategic work of the organization, and it provides a framework around which to build an action-oriented work plan for enhancing your organization's effectiveness. Evaluation is a starting point to help you determine how your organization can be more successful in achieving its overall mission.

*Nonprofits should think about evaluation
in terms of real program development—as a way
to set goals and measurements, as a key aspect of
how you create a program that makes sense.*

—Unmi Song, Executive Director
Lloyd A. Fry Foundation

Evaluation is part of program development. It is difficult to build on success if you are not sure whether you are really experiencing success. Although new ideas for programmatic initiatives bubble up every day, those that are most likely to work are those with some basis in experience and analysis. If you are about to apply for a major grant or invest in a new program that is an offshoot of something you've done before, you want to make the case that the program you did before was incredibly valuable and netted real results. You want to make sure that you're not developing an offshoot based on a trunk that is weak or on assumptions that have no demonstrable basis in reality.

As Marcia Lipetz, president and CEO of the Executive Service Corps of Chicago, puts it, "What do you really know about your program? How do you know that you know what you know? Evaluation helps lay the groundwork for programs that have a greater chance at being successful."

Understanding Potential Risks and Rewards

Evaluation is critical to your ongoing work, but it is not a cure-all. It doesn't eliminate the need for ongoing decision making or substitute for the exercise of good judgment on a day-to-day basis. Launching an evaluation process involves some risk: collecting data might be more difficult than imagined; plans can disintegrate; the organization might learn something it doesn't want to hear. And what is learned will need to be addressed, which may be time-consuming and require additional resources and energy.

On the flip side, successful, completed evaluations often astonish and re-energize stakeholders in wonderful ways. Evaluation can motivate and inspire your board, staff, donors, clients, and the local community.

SUPPORTING STEPS FOR UNDERSTANDING EVALUATION

☐ *Examine what's happening within the sector as a whole.* Note what's happening relative to legal requirements, governance, and accountability. A simple way to do this is periodically to check in with your local association of nonprofits or grantmakers or log on to the Web site of Independent Sector (www.independentsector.org) or the Web site of the National Council of Nonprofit Associations (www.ncna.org). Developing solid evaluation efforts now will help you prepare for whatever changes may be ahead.

☐ *Lay the groundwork.* Make the case for evaluation in your organization. Start talking about it positively (instead of negatively, if that's been the habit around your organization). Talk about it as a core part of everyone's work. Communicate to your board and staff leaders that the time is right for your organization to focus on evaluation in a way that it hasn't in the past. Help your board see evaluation as an expression of good management and good governance—an indicator of how well your board is attending to core duties. Help your staff see evaluation as a necessary part of ongoing planning and program development—an avenue to better achieving your mission.

☐ *Let your board and staff leaders know that you will soon be presenting a proposal.* Do this as soon as you finish reading this book! Suggest how evaluation can be incorporated into your work—ideally, your work for the coming year.

☐ *Call favorite colleagues at organizations similar to yours.* Ask for a copy of any evaluation report they've completed in the past few years. Start a file of sample evaluations. This will let you see how they tend to be alike in format and how they vary. Pass this file around at your first evaluation committee meeting.

☐ *Use sample agendas.* Sample agendas follow at the end of each chapter. Use these to help move your team step-by-step through the evaluation process. You may want to collapse or combine some agendas or adapt them to fit your needs. As a series, the six agendas offer a process to follow from start to finish. They are provided in order to give you additional guidance as you implement the steps recommended in this book.

Meeting Agenda 1
Preparing for Evaluation

Attendees: Executive Committee and Key Staff

1. REVIEW Why we're creating an evaluation committee and how this connects to priorities and concerns we identified in recent board and staff meetings.

2. DISCUSS What our history with evaluation has been in the past, what pressures are on us now, what needs we especially want to meet.

3. DECIDE Who should be on the evaluation committee, whether this should be a standing board committee, and whether there are special advisers we can invite to join us for this inaugural year who can come to a few early meetings to get us launched in the right direction.

4. NEXT STEPS Identify someone to call colleagues and get copies of "committee job descriptions" used by other evaluation committees or teams, as well as copies of any evaluation reports they'd like to share, so we can start a mini-library of sample evaluations we can refer to as models.

5. NEXT MEETING Plan for the next meeting, where we will provide a brief presentation on the evaluation process we'd like to follow. Who else should join us for that meeting? Should we also take this up at our annual retreat? It would be a great topic for the board to address.

A Simple Evaluation Framework

*N**ow that you have a greater understanding of why evaluation has become increasingly important for nonprofits, how do you begin thinking about it within the context of your own organization? This chapter discusses the basics of what, when, and how to evaluate; it also provides a framework on which to build. The concepts in this chapter are followed by more detailed how-to steps in subsequent chapters.*

Although there are many audiences that will be interested in what you learn, your evaluation is first and foremost for your leadership and your organization—to help you plan, adjust, and improve. Done right, evaluation is a process by which an organization tracks and assesses its work in order to learn more about where and why it is succeeding—or failing.

THE BASIC EVALUATION FRAMEWORK

Key to an evaluation system that is workable and sustainable for your organization is keeping the basic steps in mind and keeping it simple.

Conducting an evaluation comes down to five commonsense tasks:

1. *Planning*—identifying your evaluation focus and audience
2. *Asking*—two or three key questions you want answered

3. *Tracking*—the activities that you conduct and the signs that you're making progress toward your goals

4. *Learning*—from what you track and what it tells you

5. *Using*—the insight you gain to shape your next program

This framework contains the steps you would follow to evaluate just about anything, from the largest goal of your organization to the most program-specific strategy. You can use this five-step framework to look at the work you do or at the outcomes it generates or the impact it has over time. We will be addressing the five steps in greater detail in the following chapters, but this is the framework for all that will follow.

This basic evaluation framework is easy to use because it reflects how nonprofit organizations function and because it is applicable to your work at any stage. It helps you zero in on what you want to learn, without getting too bogged down in "what kind" of evaluation you're doing. There's a lot of jargon out there—*formative evaluation, summative evaluation, process, outcome, logic models* (see Resource B for definitions of these and other evaluation terms). But the simplest way to understand evaluation is to relate it to the fundamental pattern of how nonprofits function: there is work, there are results, and, over time, there is impact (see Exhibit 2.1). At any given time, you may want to evaluate one or more of these three dimensions.

Exhibit 2.1
The Flow of Nonprofit Work and the Nature of Evaluation

You do work. When you evaluate how well you do what you do,
it's called a *process evaluation.*

Your work has results. When you evaluate the results of your work,
it's called an *outcome evaluation.*

Lots of work produces multiple outcomes over time.
This equals *impact.*

Work produces results, and multiple results over time add up to impact. Let's look at how one of our sample organizations, the East Morgan Neighborhood Network, would describe their process, outcomes, and impact:

1. The work they do: The Network's activism is around lead poisoning, including efforts such as producing a newsletter, organizing rallies, creating educational materials. This is their *process*.

2. The result of their work: Two legislators meet with the organization's leaders and, as a result, form a subcommittee to explore hazardous lead conditions in the neighborhood; five school principals take the issue to their parents' organizations and create greater awareness; four child care centers begin lead-abatement programs. These are their *outcomes*.

3. Cumulative results: Lead poisoning is reduced by 40 percent in East Morgan after five years. This is their *impact*.

In any given evaluation cycle, you might be looking at what you do and how to do it better, or what happened as a result of your work, or both.

As we will discuss in greater detail in the chapters ahead, what you choose to look at depends on what you want to learn at any given point in your organization's history *and* what you can reasonably tackle. For smaller organizations, we recommend tackling only a couple of questions at a time and evaluating on a rolling basis. Examining one or two facets of a program in a given year, for example, works better and is more manageable than attempting to examine all of them in a monster process every five or six years.

Whether you're looking at your process (how well you do what you do) or your outcomes (the results of what you do) and how your work influences your target audience (your impact), you can plan, ask, track, learn, and use information that will help you become more powerful as an organization. The following chart (Exhibit 2.2) provides a summary of key principles to keep in mind as you consider the basic evaluation framework in light of your own organization's practices.

Exhibit 2.2
Characteristics of Less Effective and More Effective Approaches to Evaluation

Less Effective	More Effective
PLANNING	
Standing where you are and looking backward; evaluating your past work	Standing where you are and looking forward; evaluating your present work
Reconstructing from old records	Planning how you'll keep records from now on
	Incorporating an evaluation process into every new program that is launched—from the start
Seeing evaluation as a one-time "final report"	Seeing evaluation as an ongoing feedback mechanism
Asking only the questions your funder wants answered	Determining the questions you want to answer with input from board, staff, constituents, and donors
Trying to evaluate *everything;* laying out too many questions	Choosing a few key questions or assumptions that you want to examine
ASKING	
Measuring something that isn't what your core work is all about	Identifying what you really want to know and what you want to see change over time
Asking how you did against a goal that was never your mission to reach	Setting goals that are specific, measurable, attainable, relevant, and time-limited
Only attempting to measure long-term outcomes that are out of your control	Setting goals that directly relate to your organization and its program work

Exhibit 2.2
Characteristics of Less Effective and
More Effective Approaches to Evaluation, Cont'd

Less Effective	More Effective
TRACKING	
Describing activities conducted but never getting to the stage of drawing conclusions	Drawing conclusions and not being afraid to make adjustments in your program as a result
Using only the same people who are directly involved in running operations to evaluate operations	Being as objective as possible, drawing on outside perspectives, as well as insider knowledge
Developing a costly, complicated system for data collection	Looking at existing sources of information first: records, staff observations
LEARNING AND USING	
Involving staff and stakeholders only at the report stage to hear "conclusions"	Using staff and stakeholders in interpretive roles: asking what this means and what the implications may be
Assuming that just doing the evaluation is enough	Creating a process for incorporating evaluation learning into ongoing work
	Ensuring that you have dollars allocated to implement the findings
Only sharing the positive findings	Sharing successes and areas that need improvement so that everyone can learn from what you are doing

KEY CONCEPTS: WHAT TO EVALUATE
AND HOW TO GET STARTED

Before we go into greater detail on the five evaluation steps, we want to emphasize some concepts regarding what to evaluate and how to evaluate.

What to Evaluate

First, your evaluation choices can support what you are trying to achieve or communicate overall, shoring up, for example, the areas that you've defined as high priority.

You don't have to evaluate everything. You can begin by evaluating one program or one aspect of your organization. You can begin by evaluating one assumption that led you to head in a particular organizational direction. You can evaluate anything that is useful to you to evaluate: your program, a priority, your organization as a whole, the workings of your board, the strength of your strategic plan, the results of a particular grant.

Evaluate something that you want to understand better and that you want to invest in improving: your outreach efforts, your board of directors, the quality of your partnerships in the community, your financial practices, fundraising efforts, communications, program implementation, or program results—to name only some possibilities.

An ideal evaluation process

- Asks good questions, gathers good information, and shares that information
- Assesses progress in ways that lead to greater mission attainment
- Draws everyone into the process of asking what organizations and stakeholders can do to improve the effectiveness of the organization
- Nurtures a climate of trust
- Employs simple, cost-effective, user-friendly methods
- Is supported by organizational leadership

Source: Gray and Stockdill, 1995.

Tie what you are evaluating to what you identify as a high-priority area. Don't waste time asking questions that aren't important or evaluating efforts in low-priority areas (unless you've got lots of time). Identify your high-priority areas, state the outcome you are seeking in those areas, and determine how you will know if you are successful in achieving the outcomes. Your evaluation flows from there. (See the "Quick Exercise" in Exhibit 2.3.)

Exhibit 2.3
Quick Exercise: Top Priorities

At a staff or board retreat, answer the following questions:

1. Relative to our stated mission, what are the *top* two priorities we see for this organization for the next two-year period?

   Priority A: _____ ,

   which relates to this aspect of our mission: _____

   _____ .

   Priority B: _____ ,

   which relates to this aspect of our mission: _____

   _____ .

2. Which of our programs support these priorities?

3. Have we identified and written down our desired outcomes for each of these programs?

For example, if you have identified a high priority as "delivering quality dance programming at community arts centers," a specific outcome that you might seek could be "to offer ballet classes, taught by working dance professionals, in a minimum of five park district sites to a total of 100 children, ages 5–7, for 16 weeks."

Consider standards in your field as you look at what to evaluate. If one of the goals you've set for your program is to ensure that your program always keeps up with advances and best practices in its field, you may want to use industry standards as a guide for an evaluation. For example, if your organization serves youth, does your staff training include a component on understanding the relationship between age and developmental stages, as is widely recommended by youth service agencies? Are you involving youth in decisions about programming, as is increasingly the standard for your field? Or, if you are evaluating the effectiveness of your organization's governance, have you reviewed the Independent Sector's list of ten things that all boards of directors should do on a regular basis?

In sum, you are free to choose what to evaluate based on what you want to learn. Many factors will contribute to your choice of evaluation questions. Perhaps you are considering closing out a particular program or campaign and heading in a new direction. Perhaps there is an aspect of your work that, internally, is a constant source of confusion and controversy. Perhaps you simply want to know how well you're doing and whether your program is meeting its goals (see Exhibit 2.4).

How to Get Started

There is no single best way to do evaluation, just as there is no single approach to planning or fundraising suitable to all nonprofits. There are many approaches to evaluation and many evaluation models from which organizations may choose. Here we recommend an approach suited to the needs of smaller and more grassroots organizations—an approach that (1) doesn't cost a lot of money, (2) can be managed in-house on an ongoing basis, and (3) doesn't require a full-time, vastly experienced evaluation specialist to implement or understand.

- *Start from where you are now.* Evaluating years or decades of past work can be done, but *if you have a limited budget* and *if you have a choice,* concentrate your resources on the present, taking into consideration what you know about your past. What do you want to know at the end of the year you are *now* beginning or about the program you are *about* to launch? Although it can be useful to reflect on early origins and historical trends, evaluation tools and techniques are really better suited to the here and now.

Exhibit 2.4
What Do We Want to Learn?

If You're Interested In	Consider Looking At
PROGRAM	
How our program works; the quality of the program ("*If* we do this. . . .")	Our *own* practices and program operations; outputs (what you produce)
	What's working well; what's not working
	How closely our work aligns with industry standards or best practices in our field
Results of our program ("*Then* they will do that. . . .")	Our *community's* practices or behaviors; outcomes (what conditions change because of your work)
	Potential positive effects; potential negative effects

If You're Interested In	Consider Looking At
ORGANIZATION	
Our board	Level of engagement in their work
	Adherence to governance standards for nonprofits
	Composition, structure
Organizational capacity	Staff structure, job descriptions, budget history/growth/expense ratios
Internal operations; administration	Efficiency, timeliness, policies
	Technology
Fundraising	Strategies
	Results (revenue against costs and against *goals*)
	Stability
	Growth potential

• *Build in simple and logical ongoing strategies.* Choose strategies that enable you to evaluate your work on a *current* basis, as it is more manageable than investing in a survey of the past. Begin by stating a desired outcome and then make a list of what you would consider good signs that you are successfully achieving that outcome as you proceed. The purpose of evaluation is to help you make adjustments now and to plan for next year. If you do not have the capacity to invest in evaluating what you did in the past, start from where you are and build as you go forward. Encourage your staff and board to see evaluation as ongoing. The answer to "when?" to evaluate to some extent then becomes "always."

• *Define the time period that's logical to you.* Anyone who has ever tried to fit a summary of program "results" into a set time period defined by a funder, or a by fiscal year, knows that programs don't always wrap up neatly by a particular calendar date. Given that you need to begin and end somewhere, however, you do need to impose some timetable on what you're looking at, if only to be able to compare what happened in one period to another.

Throughout this book, we talk about the evaluation cycle as a yearly cycle, taking place within a twelve-month period. If your program is better suited to a longer evaluation cycle, say, eighteen or twenty-four months, that's fine. The point is to get in the habit of evaluating your work on an ongoing basis rather than "doing evaluation" once every five or ten years.

• *Build the cost of evaluation into your annual budget.* Evaluation can be done on a shoestring, with minimal resources and no additional staff other than the staff you've got, but that is not ideal. If you can get funding for your evaluation, if you can bring in a consultant even once or twice to help you plan, that's terrific. Whatever its anticipated costs, begin building those costs into your annual budget now.

• *Begin by making sure that your goals for the programs you want to evaluate are clear.* Evaluation begins with understanding explicitly what you hope to achieve. Be clear about what your goals are at the beginning; it is very difficult to evaluate something if there is no agreement as to what its goal was in the first place. It might be "obvious" to you, especially if you are the program's creator, but it might not be so obvious to the person who has your job two years from now and is trying to figure out what you were thinking.

• *You do not need to ask a thousand questions.* Neither do you need to describe in comprehensive detail every single aspect of your program. You are not writing a novel. You can ask one question—one very good question—and collect information over the year to help you answer it. You can set one goal, decide what might be good signs that you are reaching that goal, and look at how you're doing. As you review the goals you have defined, keep in mind that as a general rule of thumb, it is best to limit yourself to no more than three goals per program area.

THE ROLLING EVALUATION METHOD

One of the struggles that smaller groups and grassroots organizations often have relative to evaluation is the overwhelming feeling that they need to evaluate *everything,* that they need to be comprehensive if the evaluation is to be legitimate and meaningful. This is neither true nor realistic. Instead, we want you to think about evaluation in terms of questions you ask and answer over time.

We recommend that organizations with limited budgets and modest capacity begin with what we call *rolling evaluation*—a method that allows you to build evaluation into your work at a manageable pace and to measure and track certain program outcome results year after year so that you can begin to demonstrate improvement over time.

Rolling evaluation means choosing one or two questions you want to explore in any given year that relate to a desired outcome and focusing that year's evaluation on that topic *only* rather than attempting a more comprehensive evaluation. Each year, one to two new evaluation questions can be added (and some dropped) so that you are rounding out the picture and accumulating knowledge about your work steadily over time. The questions added each year may be variations on the previous year's question (for example, "Compared to last year, how did this program perform?"). They may be questions about another aspect of the program or they may be wholly new questions related to issues that arise.

Continue some questions as you fold in and drop out others. You do not necessarily need to ask a different question every year, because you may want to compare this year's crop of apples to next year's crop of apples for a number of years running. However, rolling evaluation allows you to plan for and fold in new questions as you are able, and to do it in a way that is manageable.

Approaching evaluation this way gets organizations into the habit of thinking evaluatively, even if formal evaluation steps are not undertaken in all areas at all times. A rolling evaluation system enables you to

1. Build evaluation into your ongoing operations on a reasonable scale.
2. Project an evaluation calendar and show funders and constituents that you

have a reasoned and manageable approach to evaluation, even if the specific area they're interested in is not "up for evaluation" this year.

3. Build up a multifaceted picture of how various pieces of your program or organization are working.

4. Compare program and organizational performance toward goals over time and understand longer-term outcomes.

We recommend that you keep a running list of the specific organizational or program-related outcomes you might want to track over the next four or five years, as well as the questions you need to ask in order to understand your progress toward those outcomes. However, do not attempt to evaluate on multiple tracks simultaneously if your organization is too small to do so.

For an organization operating on a smaller scale, a rolling evaluation system helps you do what you can this year and collect information on what you know you're going to want to explore next year. It enables you to think ahead and to let stakeholders know that you have a well considered plan that is intended to help you answer important questions, but answer them over time in a way that fits your capacity.

Questions that might be identified as part of a rolling evaluation calendar, created by our friends at Democracy Begins Here, for example, are shown in Exhibit 2.5.

In the example calendar, are the questions being posed suggestive of a "process evaluation" or an "outcome evaluation"? There are elements typical of one and some elements typical of the other, but which term applies should not overly concern you. We discuss the distinction between process evaluation and outcome evaluation so that you understand the difference, and because these are terms you are likely to hear from funders and others as you continue your work. However, when you are thinking about what to evaluate, you should think about what you want to know and not worry about what kind of evaluation your question might imply.

In the example in Exhibit 2.5, board members at Democracy Begins Here did not sit around and discuss whether they wanted a process or outcome evaluation. A group of leaders within the organization was pushing for more dollars to be invested in the organization's training program; they needed more information. Hence, they decided to evaluate training programs before investing more money.

Exhibit 2.5
Example of a Calendar of Rolling Evaluation Questions

QUESTIONS SCHEDULED FOR ROLLING EVALUATION

Priority Area: Parent Leadership Development

Desired Overall Outcome for This Priority Area: Strong working partnerships between parents, community members, and individual schools become standard in the school district decision-making process.

TIME FRAME	THE QUESTION WE'LL EXPLORE
2006–2007	Are our parent leaders benefiting from the training we provide? How do we know? How can we improve our training?
2008–2009	Are we retaining parent involvement over time? Is the number of parents involved in the school increasing? Are parents aware of our issues and our resources?
2010–2011	How do school district personnel regard our parent members? Are they seen as partners? As adversaries?

Evaluation should be a key element in your planning and decision making. The running list of evaluation questions you will tackle can be developed as part of your ongoing strategic and annual planning. When a constituent, colleague, or funder then asks, "How do you know that program is working?" you can share informal observations and indicators of how things are going, and you can legitimately reassure your supporters that the area in which they are particularly interested is, in fact, on the docket for the current five-year evaluation period and will be addressed specifically at a particular time.

When all is said and done, everyone wants to know whether or not your program is having any impact. Apart from the fact that rolling evaluation is more manageable than larger-scale evaluations, this approach emphasizes an important point relative to impact: the fact that impact is cumulative, that it cannot be discerned in short measures or trusted in quick fixes, and that success has many "mothers."

By evaluating multiple streams of work over a rolling time frame, you create a multifaceted picture that helps you to see connections and relationships between parts. As you proceed with your rolling evaluation, tackling an ever-expanding list of related questions year by year, what you learn *over time* will provide the best evidence of the overall impact your program is having.

SUPPORTING STEPS FOR THE
BASIC EVALUATION FRAMEWORK

☐ Rather than thinking of evaluation as the test that follows the work, begin to think of evaluation as the measures you put in place beforehand to help you run your programs. How will you evaluate the work you're planning for this year, or next year?

☐ Review the chart called "Characteristics of Less Effective and More Effective Evaluations" (Exhibit 2.2), which summarizes some of the key concepts in the evaluation framework described at the beginning of this chapter. Share this chart with your evaluation team.

☐ Use the sample agenda to introduce and discuss with your team the evaluation process you're hoping to follow; the sample can also help you set a meeting schedule and begin discussing needs, roles, and responsibilities.

Meeting Agenda 2
Preparing for Evaluation

Attendees: Staff

1. REVIEW Highlights of last board discussion.

2. DISCUSS Present an overview of the basic idea of rolling evaluation, which we'd like to institute at our organization. Highlights based on *Level Best* include

- Evaluation as a planning tool

- Looking to where we'll be next year, rather than where we were last

- Evaluating against specific and clearly defined goals

- Framework of Planning, Asking, Tracking, Learning, Using

- Projecting a calendar of evaluation questions but not tackling too many at once. What are staff questions and concerns?

3. DECIDE What we need to know in order to begin. Identify staff and board leaders who will participate in evaluation decision making.

4. NEXT STEPS Circulate *Level Best* to staff so all have a sense of what we're talking about doing. In preparation for determining what to evaluate, program staff should generate a list of one- or two-sentence goal statements for all the key program activities they conduct. (See Exhibit 2.3.) Do not write lengthy essays full of vague or abstract phrases. Generate as concise a goal checklist as possible. Include it as a handout at board retreat.

5. NEXT MEETING Executive committee to plan agenda for board retreat.

Planning Your Evaluation

*Y*ou've made a commitment to evaluation—perhaps even provided a new vision of evaluation for board and staff leaders—and now you're ready to start planning. This chapter outlines considerations you need to factor into your planning in order to ensure that you end up with the type of information most useful to your organization. It provides a step-by-step guide to writing your evaluation plan.

A QUICK REVIEW OF BASIC ORGANIZATIONAL READINESS

We've stressed that evaluation should be a strategy for looking ahead and that you should start from where you are. As you begin planning the ways in which you'll incorporate evaluation into your work, you will want to look at the health and status of your organization. You don't need to have a "perfect" organization to come to agreement on annual goals and a plan for your evaluation. Not all of the elements listed below need to be in place for you to begin planning, but the more they are, the easier your task.

You have or soon will have in place the following:

- A clear organizational mission
- Internal clarity and agreement as to the need for evaluation
- Commitment on the part of key staff and the board to undertake and manage the evaluation
- A generally healthy organizational base, that is, you are not in extreme turmoil or on the brink of collapse

- A solid board with an engaged, connected board chair
- A capable executive director with at least twelve months on the job
- Basic computer systems
- A recently completed strategic plan for the organization
- A history of community support
- Funding, if needed, to carry out the evaluation and implement what is learned
- Consensus on a few priority areas that will become the initial focus of your rolling evaluation
- A sense of what you want to know about your work and how are you going to use what you learn

DEFINITION OF AN EFFECTIVE ORGANIZATION

According to an internal memo at Chicago Grantmakers for Effective Organizations:

An effective nonprofit organization fulfills its mission, communicates its vision and mission, plans for the future, achieves and measures results, manages an active and informed governance structure, secures resources appropriate to needs, and engages and serves its community.

As you consider your readiness to take on evaluation and your overall organizational health, consult the chart that follows (Exhibit 3.1), which outlines the characteristics and practices typical of effective nonprofits. Use the chart as a framework for a staff or board retreat, and check how your organization looks against these recommended standards. Because you can evaluate any aspect of your work, depending on your needs and priorities, this overview will help you to identify areas on which your organization may want to focus its initial evaluation efforts.

By now, you know you need to do evaluation, but you may be worried that you do not have resources sufficient to take it on.

Chances are, *you already evaluate your work.* On a modest scale, perhaps, without coordinating all the pieces, but on some level you are most likely engaged in some of the steps you would need to take to conduct an evaluation. Ask yourself these questions:

Are you holding staff meetings and discussing where you're succeeding and where changes might need to be made?

Exhibit 3.1
Characteristics of Less and More Effective Nonprofits

Less Effective	More Effective
MISSION, VISION, PROGRAM	
Prompted by individual, charitable impulse	Prompted by thoughtful, collective decisions
Program shaped exclusively by service *providers*	Program shaped equally by service *recipients*
View of work is broad; mission is vague	Mission is clear, strategic, niche-specific
Tends to serve private interest of individual founder(s)	Clearly focused on serving public interest
Programs don't tie into mission	Clarity of mission seen in programs
TEAM, STRUCTURE, GOVERNANCE	
Board and staff roles unclear and melded	Board and staff roles defined and separate
Board micromanages all functions, even after start-up phase is over	Board sees chief duties as policy setting, overall stewardship, and financial health
Volunteer development haphazard	Volunteers trained, managed, rewarded
Board believes policies are "implicit"	Board makes policies "explicit," in writing
Decision making dominated by founders or other small groups of stakeholders	Decision making done by board as whole, following established channels and protocols
Board gets involved in hiring all staff	Board only hires executive director, who hires others
Does not keep up with nonprofit standards or follow widely recommended best practices	Regularly consults and updates policies and practices
Nominations are eccentric and random	Nominations process follows clearly established procedures

Exhibit 3.1
Characteristics of Less and More Effective Nonprofits, Cont'd

Less Effective	More Effective
RESOURCE DEVELOPMENT, FINANCIAL MANAGEMENT, OPERATIONS	
Budgeting often begins with what the organization thinks it can or should *spend*	Budgeting begins with assessment of needs and with what the organization thinks it can or should *raise*
Organization regularly spends outside budget	Organization uses budget as management tool
Fundraising is scattershot, whimsical, afterthought; often heavy reliance on a few core donors	Fundraising is staffed, annualized, maintained by clear systems and multiple strategies
Organization hesitant to invest in fundraising, infrastructure, or communications; fears spending on anything but program	Organization understands it must invest in itself to survive and grow; to publicize and deliver programs properly, and to reach out to new constituents
Sees fundraising only as means to budget goal	Also sees fundraising as public education and communications, a way to reinforce program
Exclusive reliance on government and foundation grants	Individual contributors also part of the mix, as well as earned income, corporate support
Few board members make financial contributions, think volunteering is enough	100 percent board giving, no matter what the level
Frequent crisis cash-flow borrowing	Short- and long-term financial planning and cash-management policies in place
No one reads, understands the budget or audit	Leadership oversees annual budget, understands what audit conveys
Lives within inadequacies of existing space, often tailoring program to the space	Develops facilities plan so that space can ultimately be tailored to program needs

Exhibit 3.1
Characteristics of Less and More Effective Nonprofits, Cont'd

Less Effective	More Effective
EVALUATION AND PLANNING	
Operates "on instinct" day-to-day	Operates with board-approved strategic plan
Progresses by fits and starts, project-to-project	Develops and regularly consults strategic plan; uses planning as a tool for direction setting
Sees evaluation as a one-time "final report"	Sees evaluation as an ongoing feedback mechanism
Asks only the evaluation questions that a funder wants answered	Determines the questions to answer with input from board, staff, constituents, and donors
Describes activities conducted but never gets to the stage of drawing conclusions	Draws conclusions and makes adjustments in program as a result
Uses only the same people who are directly involved in running operations to evaluate operations	Is as objective as possible, drawing on outside perspectives as well as insider knowledge

Source: Adapted from Festen and Philbin, 2002, p. 26.

Are you in touch with your audience members, clients, or constituents and listening to what they have to say?

Are you making notes in the middle of the night about what might help them even more?

Is someone keeping track of how many people come through your doors?

Are you observing your programs in action?

Do program staff or funders or friends of the organization occasionally share their observations and reflections with the executive director, perhaps even in writing?

People evaluate all the time—the movies they see, the food they eat, the relationships they have at home and at work. What you're doing may be informal or erratic, but if you are engaging in any of these activities, you are already engaged in evaluation.

The evaluation process that you will put in place involves formalizing similar steps and strategies. The formal process is an attempt to establish an organizational habit of regularly asking questions about and tracking your work.

But who, you may be wondering, would actually conduct the evaluation? Chances are, you don't have enough people to do your day-to-day work, let alone take on something new. Few small organizations have the luxury of a full-time staff person whose job it is to oversee evaluation. As is the case for much that needs tending to in nonprofit organizations, the responsibility for evaluation is usually shared—just like the responsibility for fundraising, planning, or public relations.

If evaluations have not been formally conducted in the past, however, determining who is going to do it and whether or not to hire a consultant to help you is one of the first decisions that need to be made.

- *If you can afford ongoing contractual help,* you might want to consider contracting with a consultant or contractual part-timer with whom you can imagine working over a period of years. With that person's assistance, you can design basic systems for regularly tracking your work and gradually build into permanent job descriptions the responsibilities that will help your organization track and evaluate on an ongoing basis.

Assuming limited funding for a consultant, consider using that expert's time to focus one of two ways: (1) on identifying the best approach to evaluation for your organization and helping to determine what records your staff should keep on a regular basis, or to develop tools for collecting the information or (2) on providing objective insight into the information you collect and analyze. Devoting consultant resources in either of these ways should maximize your return.

For the data collection itself, you can look internally or to volunteers to apply the methods you decide to use, for example, conducting interviews, sending out and analyzing results of questionnaires, and so on.

- *If you can afford one-time contractual help,* consider hiring an evaluation professional to help you get your house in order, so to speak, by helping you create and install the systems, storage, habits, and procedures that will help you keep what you need accessible and manageable.
- *If you are operating on a do-it-yourself basis,* don't worry. It can be done, and it can be done well. Begin by identifying one or two board members or volunteers who you think could positively contribute and who will agree to be part of an internal evaluation team. Next, review staff job descriptions and determine what kinds of record-keeping logically fall into which job descriptions. Review board committee job descriptions and be explicit about which team should be responsible for monitoring evaluation. Make use of local nonprofit library resources, attend evaluation trainings, or ask a foundation program officer or nonprofit colleague who understands evaluation to assist you in identifying your approach and methods. Follow the steps in this book, and customize the agendas, forms, and materials for your own use.

The most difficult part of conducting an evaluation *completely* in-house is that there is a strong chance that the information gathered about strengths and weaknesses will be difficult to interpret objectively if the people responsible for implementing the work are also responsible for assessing it. It is hard to look over your own shoulder. So, if possible, either have someone within the organization *other than the program manager* look at the results, or identify a volunteer with an objective view who is willing to serve on an evaluation committee or as a special adviser. This person can be a board member, the colleague of a board member, a graduate student from a local university, a retired executive, or a panel of "critical friends" from other nonprofits in your field whom you know and trust and who are supporters of your organization.

WHAT YOU PLAN AFFECTS WHAT YOU LEARN

The process and plan you use for your evaluation will ultimately influence what you learn from it. If your motivation is simply to fulfill requirements set by a funder, you're unlikely to learn much. The chart in Table 3.1 suggests the range of learning that is possible, depending on what assumptions and plans you make at the outset.

Table 3.1
The Evaluative Learning Continuum

Key Questions	Zero-to-Minimal Learning	Modest Learning	Significant Learning	High Learning
1. What's the purpose of the evaluation?	Accountability to funders	Accountability to funders and organizational leaders	Program planning	Organizational and program planning
2. Who is the audience for the findings?	Funders	Funders and organizational leaders	Funders, organizational leaders, and staff	Funders, organizational leaders, staff, and the broader field
3. Who will conduct the evaluations?	External evaluator	External evaluator (hired by funders) with assistance from organizational staff	External evaluator (hired by organization) in conjunction with organizational staff	Internal evaluator, perhaps with coaching from an external evaluator, if not trained in evaluation
4. Who will determine the evaluation questions and evaluation design process?	Funders and external evaluator	Funders, external evaluators, and organizational leaders	Funders, external evaluators, organizational leaders, and staff	Funders, external evaluators, organizational leaders, staff and community stakeholders
5. What data are available to address evaluation questions?	Objective data gathering using only scientific methods	Objective data gathering using only scientific or quasi-scientific methods	Objective and subjective data	Objective, subjective, and alternative types of data (for example, pictures or stories)

6. What types of evaluation reports or presentations of data are provided?	Very detailed findings but no examination of recommendations beyond the data	Somewhat detailed, with some examination of recommendations beyond the data	User-friendly (that is, audience-defined), with examination of recommendations beyond the data	User-friendly (that is, audience-defined), with examination of recommendations beyond the data, and incorporates a reflective process (for example, program-planning "scenarios")
7. Who will provide interpretive feedback on the findings?	Funders	Funders and organizational leaders	Funders, organizational leaders, and staff	Funders, organizational leaders, staff, clients, community stakeholders, and the broader field
8. How frequently will evaluations occur?	At the conclusion of program funding	At the conclusion of each program cycle	Periodically throughout the life of the program	Ongoing for all programs within the organization

Source: York, 2003, p. 5.

STEP BY STEP: PLANNING YOUR EVALUATION

Here are steps you can follow to make a plan for the front end of the evaluation process.

Step 1: Conduct Board and Staff Orientation

If you have not recently done an evaluation at your organization, you will want to begin by ensuring that your leaders understand the evaluation philosophy and vocabulary in the same way and are ready to make whatever the financial and organizational commitment may be. Likewise, if you have experience conducting evaluations but want to make some changes in your evaluation budget, perspective, or structure, you will still need to do some advance work with board and staff.

Questions to consider discussing at this stage: Why are we undertaking an evaluation? Who in particular has "asked" for it? What is the board's role? How will we use it? How much can we afford to invest in it? When will we follow up?

Step 2: Determine Roles and Job Responsibilities

Who's in charge? If record keeping for evaluation is part of one (or more) staff member's responsibilities, is it specifically included in his or her job description? Do job descriptions need to be adjusted? Will outside help be needed? Is there a board committee that relates to the evaluation process?

At small nonprofits, volunteers and the board play crucial roles, and an evaluation team should be considered to provide support and coordination. At the end of this chapter, you'll find a sample agenda you can use to help your evaluation team navigate the process and set some evaluation goals and parameters.

Step 3: Identify What You Are Already Doing

As we mentioned earlier, if you are holding staff retreats to discuss program challenges, keeping records, filing reports, clipping newspaper stories on the events you've sponsored in your community, or even taking photographs of programs in action, you are already gathering data and engaging in a kind of evaluation. Think about how these efforts can be used in a more formal evaluation process.

Step 4: Develop a Time Frame

You need to make two decisions about time frame. First, you need to determine the period of time you will be examining. If you are looking at past efforts, clarify whether you're evaluating your program since inception or during the last twelve months or some other time period. If you're looking to evaluate what you'll be doing in the coming year or years, determine the intended outcomes you want to measure and what block of time you need to measure them.

Second, you need to decide the calendar for your evaluation process or cycle, including the amount of time you will allocate to conducting it.

Step 5: Develop a Budget

Ideally, evaluation should become part of the standard cost of running your program and organization. Different evaluation plans and strategies vary in terms of how expensive they are, and organizations may have legitimate reasons for using multiple strategies. Overall, however, evaluation costs range from 5 to 10 percent of the program's or organization's costs.

Step 6: Clarify Your Overarching Goals for Each Program or Initiative You Want to Evaluate

You cannot evaluate a program that has no set goals. If there are no explicit, written goals, you have no criteria against which to judge the program. Make sure you have this for each program or initiative you want to evaluate.

Step 7: Zero in on the Questions You Want Your Evaluation to Explore

With your leadership team, you will want to spend some time figuring out what you want to investigate. Begin by brainstorming the questions that you might want to answer as related to your stated goals, and then narrow down the list of possible questions to the one or two you will tackle first.

Step 8: Commit the Plan to Paper

The fill-in-the-blank worksheet that follows (Worksheet 3.1) will help you put all the pieces together. If you work with your "evaluation team" to answer these questions, you essentially will have created the blueprint for your evaluation, a document that will guide you as you move ahead with subsequent steps. Drafts should be circulated throughout the organization, with a comment sheet that can be used to gather input and suggestions for revisions. Staff can judge its feasibility. The board's full support is needed. In the end, the entire board and staff ideally needs to agree on it. (A completed "Sample Evaluation Planning Worksheet" can be found in Resource C.)

Worksheet 3.1
Evaluation Planning Worksheet

Organization name: _____

Date: _____

SUMMARY

Evaluation focus for this year (dates): _____

The focus of our evaluation for this year is to determine whether/ prepare for/gain insight into . . . *because.* . . .

(Example: "This year we will look at our suburban youth program because we are losing our suburban partner and must decide whether to continue on our own.")

The questions we will ask to learn what we want to know are:

1. (Example: "How do other youth programs in that suburb view our presence there? What unique value do we bring?")

2.

Worksheet 3.1
Evaluation Planning Worksheet, Cont'd

Check the box that applies:

The evaluation goal indicated above means we are evaluating:

☐ A *priority,* or priority area, or an aspect of our mission as a whole

☐ A piece of our *organization,* one of the structures that enable our work

☐ A particular *program*

☐ An aspect of a program, a *strategy* within a program area

☐ A specific *grant*

The block of time we'll look at is from _____ **to** _____.

We will evaluate the activity that takes place in this area during that period of time.

Description (brief history of program or area to be evaluated):

The condition we're addressing through this program or function is:

The desired overall outcome or goal for this program or function is:

Worksheet 3.1
Evaluation Planning Worksheet, Cont'd

Methods (how we'll gather information to answer our questions)

To answer Evaluation Question 1 (which is "_____

_____

_____?")

we will track the following:

Measure 1: _____

Measure 2: _____

Measure 3: _____

We will measure this using the following techniques (check all that apply):

☐ Record review:

☐ Observation of:

☐ Interviews of:

☐ Focus group(s) with:

☐ Survey(s) of:

☐ Other:

(Copy this page and fill in the same information for your Evaluation Question 2.)

Worksheet 3.1
Evaluation Planning Worksheet, Cont'd

USES/DISSEMINATION

Once completed, we will share the results of this evaluation with:

___ Board and staff

___ Funder(s): _____

___ Other: _____

We will use it to:

___ Plan for next year

___ Other: _____

RESPONSIBILITIES:

_____ will be responsible for the management and oversight of all evaluation activities, including convening staff and board teams to review plans, progress, findings, and implications.

_____ will be responsible for data collection.

_____ will be responsible for data analysis and reporting.

_____ will review and edit the final report.

The liaison or board committee for evaluation consists of: _____
_____

The final report is to be completed by _____

We have allocated $ _____ toward the anticipated costs of this evaluation, which include mailings for surveys, food for meetings, and fees.

UNDERSTANDING FUNDERS' NEEDS AND FITTING THEM INTO YOUR EVALUATION PLAN

Funders may ask for it in different ways, but they all want basically the same thing: *something to go on besides blind faith.* They want something that summarizes for them, in a legitimate and relatively comprehensive way, both what you did and why you think it mattered. Too often, grantee organizations (especially small organizations) either submit to funders a list of activities or tasks completed, leaving funders to draw their own conclusions, or they claim sweeping and significant results, without explaining how the organization achieved them.

Funders want to understand: (1) what your organization is attempting to do and (2) what it is achieving. In order to do so, they want reports that sum it up for them as neatly and objectively as possible.

Different funders behave differently in response to evaluation and offer varying reasons for wanting evaluation from grantees. Usually, public funders (including the United Way) are, in effect, spending other people's money—whether it is tax dollars or donations. Public funders have a strong need for transparency and accountability.

GRANT REPORTS VERSUS EVALUATIONS

What's the difference between a foundation's required year-end grant report and an evaluation?

Foundation grant reports require you to answer questions about a specific grant you received and share information that indicates whether the goals of the grant were met. (Were funds spent as agreed? Did you accomplish what you said you would? What were the results? What was learned from this grant?) Each foundation asks for a grant report in order to understand the effectiveness of its own grantmaking and to ensure grantee accountability.

Evaluation, however, is not typically focused on a single grant, or funding period. Rather, it is an ongoing process of learning that helps you understand what difference your work makes and provides insights on how to improve or build, based on what you learn.

Private funders typically are using grantee evaluation results to back up their own hypotheses, assess their own impact as grantmakers, and determine future investments. Many foundations are becoming more demanding in terms of what they require from grantseekers in a proposal submission or at the application stage, as well as in the reports that grantees are expected to submit after a grant is made.

Just as nonprofits are under pressure to identify the results of their programs, private foundations are under pressure to justify their own grantmaking strategies and investments. Foundations often assess their own impact based on the grants they make.

Much of what private funders require in proposals in the form of "evaluation plans" is intended to be preventative. Many funders have learned the hard way that it is better to ask a potential grantee up front exactly what outcomes they expect and then to measure performance against that, rather than to wait, return to the grantee a year later, and find a hodge-podge of claimed results that don't particularly relate to anything the funder was interested in supporting in the first place.

In short, funders want you to do what they're going to be asked to do: to describe your work and to draw some conclusions. A good evaluation does both.

You may be wondering, "How can I choose just one or two evaluation questions when my funders want me to evaluate every grant?"

The one or two overarching questions you choose may end up generating information that answers a variety of smaller or more grant-specific questions, or they may show how the work that one particular grant supported fits into the larger context of what a program is accomplishing overall.

However, even as you plan your evaluation and pursue insight into the main area you are exploring with your evaluation this cycle, you can take steps to monitor other programs, too. Evaluating one area does not mean turning your back on all others. For example, you can make sure you are maintaining good records on your other activities and reporting back to funders as required. You also can take steps to ensure that the purpose of each grant is clear and that each supports specific desired outcomes.

WHY SETTING GOALS MAKES EVALUATION EASIER

Program plans that set specific goals can more easily be evaluated and make both planning and evaluation easier.

For example, so that it can evaluate its arts grants according to goals set by each grant seeker (as opposed to evaluate against some other, more mysterious standard), The Chicago Community Trust (The Trust) asks that proposals be submitted in a format that makes grant and program evaluation fairly simple. (For more information, see the group's Web site, www.cct.org.)

In a process developed by senior program officer Kassie Davis, applicants for grants to the Trust are asked to state their "hopes" in terms of specific outcomes that The Trust grant would help the group achieve. Specifically, grant applicants are asked to identify no more than three intended outcomes per grant and no more than two "measures" that would help determine what kind of progress is being made toward achieving that outcome.

Stating your priorities in terms of specific outcomes that you intend to achieve may make initial organizational planning a little more intensive, but it makes subsequent evaluation and follow-up planning a great deal easier—for fundraising staff and for program staff. Imagine the headaches a staff member endures when trying to put together a final report on an arts grant when the proposal only broadly states that "this season will be better than ever" or "we hope to attract larger and larger audiences." Then imagine how the final report might be assembled if the proposal were built on specifics such as these:

> *Desired outcome:* Our theater's main stage audience engagement increases.
>
> *How we'll know we're making progress* (Measure 1): Main stage attendance as a percent of capacity will increase to 65 percent for the 2006-2007 season.
>
> *How we'll know we're making progress* (Measure 2): 90 percent of main stage audience members completing the end of season survey will be "very" or "somewhat satisfied" with the 2005–06 season.

Defining desired outcomes in this specific manner helps with annual planning; it also creates a relatively easy way for staff leaders to provide periodic progress reports to board committees and for the board to follow what the organization is doing in a concrete fashion.

HOW YOU CAN PREPARE

The program staff at foundations that support your organization may be able to provide you with resources, support, and expertise in designing your evaluation. Many foundations have invested significant amounts of their own time and money in learning about what makes effective evaluation, and some provide technical assistance and other support to grantees in need of evaluation advice.

Exhibit 3.2 provides examples of questions asked by different foundations at the conclusion of a grant period. Review the examples to get an understanding of the types of evaluation information funders often look for. Thinking about how you might answer these questions can help you anticipate considerations that might influence your evaluation planning.

Exhibit 3.2
What Funders Ask

The Polk Bros. Foundation Grantee Annual Follow-Up Report

Please give a brief overview of the program funded by the grant.

Please compare the program carried out with the grant proposal. What were the differences? If changes or omissions were made, briefly explain the reasons.

Discuss the accomplishments of the program. Please list stated objectives, if applicable, and note progress toward meeting those objectives.

Please describe any difficulties that occurred in carrying out the program. If you were unable to accomplish certain objectives, what hindered progress?

What are the conclusions of your assessment of the program, and what program changes do you plan as a result?

What is your assessment of the impact of the program on the underlying problem you sought to address?

The Crossroads Fund Grantee Progress Report

Questions for Evaluating, Gauging Impact, and Measuring Effectiveness of Your Work

List one key organizational accomplishment (a success, victory, outcome) during the period covered by this report.

What were the results?

How does that accomplishment relate to your organization's mission?

How will you build on that success?

Please give concrete examples of the impact of the grant in the community you serve (that is, increased community interest, dialogue, and participation; involved community members in decision making; developed leadership among constituency; signs of changing cultural norms, and so on).

Exhibit 3.2
What Funders Ask, Cont'd

Please give concrete examples of your work's impact on the issue(s) you are addressing, that is, challenging and changing public policy and practices, challenging and changing institutional policies and practices, building strong alliances and coalitions, getting media coverage, raising community awareness.

What challenges/barriers have you encountered in meeting the goals of your work (for example, leadership changes, policy setbacks, organizational capacity needs)? How did you handle them?

What types of organizational capacity-building needs, if any, do you have? How are you currently addressing them?

With which other organizations or coalitions did you collaborate during the period of this report? Briefly describe how you worked with them. What was your reason for collaborating with them?

Were there any lessons learned (methods, strategies, organizational issues) in carrying out your activities? Would this change the way you do your work? How?

Describe key fundraising efforts and outcomes during this grant period, including successes and failures. Did the Crossroads Fund grant help in securing additional funding?

Source: Crossroads Fund, Chicago: Polk Bros. Foundation, 2006.

SUPPORTING STEPS FOR
PLANNING YOUR EVALUATION

☐ Circulate the fill-in-the-blank Evaluation Planning Worksheet from this chapter to your evaluation team so that everyone knows what needs to be addressed in a plan.

☐ Make sure there is agreement and clarity about your mission and goals. The most important aspect of planning is choosing your evaluation question (which is discussed in greater detail in the next chapter).

Before you can choose your question, you need to make sure your mission and program goals are clear. In all evaluations, it is important to continually refer back to your fundamental mission in order to make sure that (to use the old expression) your focus on the trees does not make it difficult to see the forest.

☐ Use the Sample Meeting Agenda that follows to fill in the blanks if you need to write, rewrite, or polish your mission statement. We've designed this discussion as a board retreat, helping to establish buy-in and support for your evaluation work.

Meeting Agenda 3
Focusing Our Mission and Our Evaluation Priorities

Attendees: Board and staff at board retreat

1. REVIEW Revisit the mission. Is our mission statement an accurate and up-to-date reflection of our work? If not, we'll work together to fill in the blanks below.

Mission Exercise:
Mission statements can be written in many different styles but should be no more than a couple of sentences and should contain the following pieces of information:

The (organization name)

Is (basic description of kind of organization)

Which works to (what it does, for whom)

Through (core programs and services).

Sample: Heartland Alliance is a service-based human rights organization focused on investments in and solutions for the most poor and vulnerable in our society. We provide housing, health care, human services, and human rights protections for people who might otherwise fall through the cracks. (Heartland Alliance, 2005)

2. DISCUSS Based on our mission, what are our top two or three priorities or goals for the next immediate time period? How would we describe our progress toward these goals?

3. DECIDE As a (grassroots/arts/community organization) concerned with (social change/arts programming/community building), how can evaluation help us more fully meet our mission and reach these goals? If we forced ourselves to rank them, in which order would they fall?

4. NEXT STEPS We identified each priority area in which we might want to consider evaluation questions *in general.* Now, without editing or debating the merits of each, work together to brainstorm a list of possible evaluation questions under each priority area, questions about our work and/or our organization that we'd love to be able to answer better.

5. NEXT MEETING Plan for the next meeting, where we will sort through that "wish list" of general questions and zero in on the few we want to explore through evaluation. Who else should join us for that meeting?

Asking the Right Questions

*T*his chapter summarizes considerations relevant to selecting your all-important evaluation question or questions. We offer strategies for sorting through the range of possibilities, as well as perspectives on what various kinds of questions tend to help organizations learn.

CLEAR PROGRAM GOALS GUIDE EVALUATION QUESTIONS AND CHOICES

You may have heard people say that evaluation can provide a "snapshot" of your work at a moment in time. Evaluation does not, in fact, provide the complete, clear view that a photograph provides. Your evaluation will only reveal elements in the precise area that you choose to examine. It is a common misperception to assume that there is something simply "there" that will become apparent if you go looking in a general way—if you aim the camera and just point and shoot.

Before you can evaluate, you need to decide what you're looking for. For every program, initiative, or aspect of your mission you want to explore and evaluate, therefore, you need to have a clear goal statement to consult. After all, it's your organization you're evaluating, and the programs you've designed flow from the ultimate goal you want to reach.

Common mistakes organizations make include

- Beginning an evaluation when goals for a program are ill-defined. Success is measured by whether or not you meet your goals; it is difficult to evaluate a program that has no set goals.

- Setting goals that are impossible to measure or achieve during the evaluation period

- Setting goals that focus solely on process (the work) or solely on outcomes (the desired results), rather than the relationship between what you do and what you hope will happen as a result
- Attempting to evaluate goals that were not really your goals in the first place or were not directly related to the work of the organization

For example, if your organization is devoted to school improvement but test scores did not rise in your district, did you fail? Not if your goal was never about test scores in the first place. What if your goal, instead, was to increase the number of neighborhood organizations working with local schools? If you did that— if you met *your* goal as opposed to someone else's goal—you succeeded. Your work should be judged against the criteria you set, and evaluated in light of the goals you are trying to reach.

Perhaps you think your goal is obvious. You run a food bank; your goal must be "feed hungry people." But a program goal is usually a bit more refined, incorporating strategy. Maybe your program goal really is to "feed hungry people in partnership with local community organizations, so that our organization builds the community's ability to meet local needs." Then you might want to look at whether the partnerships are working, as well as the number of meals served.

Likewise, a fundraising event that raises lots of money would seem to be a success in anyone's book. But what if the goal for the event was to bring in new supporters? If only two out of the two hundred attendees were new supporters, then the event did not succeed. It might have served other purposes but it missed the goal set for the event.

Let's look at another organization. Artists and Musicians for Literacy (AML) wants to help its city turn out more literate citizens. Many other organizations share this objective, from schools to corporate giving programs. The way AML works toward this end, however, is unique to AML. The organization believes that *if* it promotes volunteerism for literacy programs, *then* more people will tutor and mentor others, and more community members will learn to read.

When you consider what AML might want to evaluate, you can look at any part of that last sentence. Did AML do a good job of promoting volunteerism? Did more people sign up to tutor and mentor as a result? Did the tutoring, in fact, develop more readers in the community?

Worksheet 4.1
What Success Looks Like

QUICK EXERCISE: WHAT DOES SUCCESS LOOK LIKE?

1. Write down the name of a project or area you'd like to evaluate in the coming year: _____

   _____

2. Your goal for this project is to_____

   _____

3. List two or three things that, if they occurred, would be signs of progress—specific examples that might show that you're making progress toward the goal you stated.

   _____

   _____

   _____

4. Now ask your program staff what's being done to make the things you named happen. Summarize the strategies that will help you get there:

Here's another example.

A good goal statement from Democracy Begins Here might be *Parent engagement helps create healthy schools. If we engage more parent and community leaders in school reform efforts, then we will create stronger school communities better able to support students.*

With that goal statement, the organization can then evaluate whether or not it has engaged more parents and whether those parents are more active on local campaigns and initiatives—no matter what the outcome of those campaigns.

A bad goal statement for Democracy Begins Here might name an outcome it couldn't really claim as its own, or require data collection or analysis beyond its capacity. Thus, a bad goal statement might be, *If we engage more parent and community leaders in school reform efforts, test scores will go up.*

As much as people may want you to do it, it is extremely difficult to evaluate what you can't reach and don't control. In fact, this is the downfall of many impact-based evaluations. The nonprofit makes a far-reaching statement to a funder or supporter to "sell" a proposal (for example, *Our work with neighborhood block clubs will lower the crime rate in this area*); then the nonprofit feels committed to prove the claim through evaluation.

The best technique for combating this tendency is to develop an appropriate and accurate *if-then* statement as you articulate your "theory of change."

Draft a statement, but then keep asking yourself the question, "What needs to happen before that can happen?" Keep asking this question until you come up with an answer that is *very close* to your program work and likely also something more directly under your control. It's a way to rein in some of the related but distant outcomes. For example:

> *If we work with block clubs, then crime will go down.*
>
> What needs to happen before that can happen?
>
> *For crime to go down, people need to feel like they can safely report gang activity.*
>
> What needs to happen before that can happen?
>
> *For people to feel safe reporting gang activity, they need to know more of their neighbors and feel more a part of the community, which is known to be a factor in reducing crime.*

So the best thing to measure in this case might be the number of people who report having met at least one new neighbor as a result of participation in the program being evaluated.

WHAT TO EVALUATE: WHAT YOU DO VERSUS WHAT YOUR CONSTITUENTS DO

Here's the difference between *process evaluation* and *outcome evaluation*: in *process evaluation,* the guiding questions focus on the quality of a program's components or their implementation. A process evaluation is about *your* work and how well you do it.

In *outcome evaluation* the guiding questions focus on the extent to which a program is achieving its desired outcomes. Your work has results. When you evaluate the results of your work, you are evaluating outcomes.

The programs you operate are no doubt complex, interdependent, at various stages of development, and supported with varying resources. However, programs all have one thing in common: in some way, they seek to have an impact on a particular group of people or a particular issue. Their goal is generally to effect change. The work of your organization, therefore, is not only about what *you* do, it is about what you hope your work will lead others to do.

- *Artists for Literacy,* for example, hopes that because of its work, more people will support literacy programs by volunteering at and donating to tutoring centers.
- *Democracy Begins Here* hopes that because of its work, parents will become active in local schools.

Looking at your work in this way involves setting out an *if-then* statement that contains the basic assumptions you make between the work you do (process) and the result (outcomes) it will have. In some circles, this is referred to as your Theory of Change (Worksheet 4.2).

If Artists for Literacy makes literacy programs stronger, *then* more people will be able to read.

If Democracy Begins Here engages more parents in school improvement efforts, *then* schools will be better equipped to offer quality education.

Worksheet 4.2
Theory of Change

QUICK EXERCISE: WHAT'S YOUR THEORY OF CHANGE?

If we do this: _____

_____

_____

_____

_____

_____

_____

_____

Then we expect this to happen: _____

_____

_____

_____

_____

_____

_____

_____

That's your theory of change.

IF OR *THEN:* WHICH TO EVALUATE?

So, which part do you evaluate—*if* or *then,* process or outcome?

Your organization will fine-tune the questions you might ask according to the nature of your programs and what you want to learn, but—there are basically two possible categories into which *all* questions could be said to fall: (1) questions about what *you* do ("If we do this . . .") and (2) questions about what *change it makes* ("Then they do that . . .").

Here are two examples:

1. A question about what you do might be: "Did we offer training programs that attracted full attendance and were rated well by participants?"

2. A question about what *they* do or about effects might be: "Did participants function differently after our training, as a result of our training?"

"If" questions—questions about what you do—tend to net information about how to improve your project, your strategy, your outreach, your support, and so on. These process evaluation questions help you assess the quality of your operations.

"They" questions look at the effects of that work, or outcome evaluation, and so tend to net information about results and impact.

Any organization can lay out a system for gathering and analyzing information about "what we do" and can use that information to improve programs and services.

Process evaluation is

- Vital to healthy program functioning

- A means of understanding the subtleties of your program components and implementation, thus helping you better understand the program's impact

- Important to funders because it lets them know that you are tweaking, improving, and changing your programs

Although fine for internal improvement purposes, process evaluation (alone) won't tell you or the outside world about the outcomes of your work. For example, you may offer training programs that are well attended and rated well by participants, but if you don't know whether the participants function differently as a result of the training, then you don't know whether the training is achieving the outcome you hoped for.

Gathering data about effects even in a rudimentary way is typically more challenging and more costly than process evaluation. It is important to do what you can to measure outcomes. But it is also important to be realistic about how much you can do.

Outcome evaluation is

- Important to understanding whether your program is achieving desired results
- Permits stronger articulation to funders and other stakeholders of a program's effect on the "condition" being addressed

THE RELATIONSHIP BETWEEN EVALUATING WHAT YOU DO (PROCESS) AND WHAT THEY DO (OUTCOME)

There is, without question, interplay between a process and an outcome evaluation. For example, if we were to design an evaluation of a one-day workshop on fundraising, the *process* evaluation, which focuses on what you do, might include an evaluation form that everyone in the workshop completes. The form might include questions about the pace of a workshop, quality of the instructor, and if the actual workshop content lived up to the advertised description.

An *outcome* evaluation of the workshop would be different. It would focus on the changes that result—and might involve a survey phone call to a random sample of workshop attendees to find out how many implemented ideas and content from the workshop, how (if at all) their behavior changed as a result of the workshop, or whether they signed up for a second workshop in the series to further their professional development.

If the results of the survey reveal that the outcome goals were not reached (for example, only two people responded that they had implemented anything from the workshop), it would be important to go back to the process evaluation to examine what could be tweaked and improved in the workshop to improve its impact. That is why it is important to do both kinds of evaluation: one gives meaning to the impact data and a way to act on what is learned, and the other gives depth and substance to the process data.

It is important to know how much or how often a program is working, but equally important is to know *why* it is working when it is. Some approaches to evaluation suggest that, in fact, the *most* important information we can gain is about *why* a program is successful, since *how often* it is successful tends to be surprisingly predictable.

Research spearheaded by evaluation consultant Robert Brinkerhoff (2003) suggests that there is a predictable distribution of results in any "intervention": on average, approximately 15 percent of those who were supposed to benefit will change behaviors and get positive results; about 20 percent will not try anything new nor change at all; and 50 to 80 percent fall somewhere in the middle, perhaps trying what a program recommends and then giving up, or trying bits and pieces only. If we assume that results always spread this way, then it makes sense to look most carefully not at what a program does on average but at what it does when it functions at its best.

When considering "The Big Question" that you might ask in your evaluation, stop and discuss with your team what it might mean to look at what brought the success you're experiencing, rather than how much success you had. An organization like the West Coast Global Donors Network might ask, in other words, not "How many global donors attended our workshops over the year?" but "What made us successful when we were successful in attracting global donors, and how can we push that further?"

DETERMINE THE RIGHT QUESTIONS

To determine the "right questions," begin by asking yourself why you are undertaking an evaluation at all. Remember that, ideally, the evaluation process is about (1) reflecting on and improving your product, (2) improving your delivery, (3) better understanding your outcomes, and (4) sustaining your organization.

Reflecting On and Improving Your "Product"

Why do you do what you do? Perhaps your organization grew out of the unique vision of a set of founders, and you are charged with continuing to carry out that vision. Perhaps your organization grew out of a need identified by a particular community, and that community continues to inform and guide your work. Perhaps you have been working with the same core content for so long that you have never questioned whether what you do is the "right" thing to do. Evaluation can help you raise and address questions that are essential but often go unasked in the course of day-to-day work.

For Artists and Musicians for Literacy, for example, a series of questions that focuses on "product" might be: Are concerts and exhibits really the best way for us to raise public awareness about the importance of improving literacy? How do we know? Are there other strategies we should consider?

Improving Your Delivery

Media analyst Marshall McLuhan once famously said that "the medium is the message," meaning that content is inextricably tied to the ways in which that content is delivered and received. This is true for nonprofits as well as other sectors, but nonprofit organizations often spend much greater amounts of time figuring out content than they do in figuring out how to "deliver" that content to their audience. Small theater companies, for example, may invest in brilliant productions and keep up with the latest in stagecraft, but fall far short on audience development. Staff at grassroots or small advocacy organizations may spend hours debating the merits of their message and how it relates to the politics of others, but never assess whether it moves their agenda forward.

In all fields, developing the product is only half the battle; finding the means of distribution is the other half. For organizations with particular confidence in their "product" it may be valuable to approach evaluation not in terms of how we alter our core product but how we deliver it more effectively.

For Artists and Musicians for Literacy, questions relative to delivery might be: Were the performers we enlisted the right performers to attract the audience we wanted? Was an outdoor festival the best strategy, or would an indoor venue be better? Should we do one big concert or a series in smaller sites?

Specific questions that relate to your product and its delivery cover topics such as the following:

Planning and implementation issues: How well was the program or initiative planned out, and how well was that plan put into practice? What do we know about the quality of our program? Possible questions:

Who participates?

Is there diversity among participants?

Are we reaching the type of person we designed this initiative for?

Why do people participate or drop out of the programs?

Are community members satisfied with our efforts?

Did we raise the money we anticipated needing for the program?

If not, what adjustments did we have to make, and what did that mean for the original program goals?

Were your speakers, staff, materials, and programs of high quality?

A possible way to answer those questions: use a monitoring system that tracks actions and accomplishments related to bringing about the mission of the initiative, such as member surveys, and staff interviews.

Meeting basic objectives: How well has the program or initiative met its stated objectives? Possible questions:

How many people participated?

Was their attrition or growth beyond what was anticipated?

How many hours are participants involved?

What major changes or alterations occurred during the course of the work?

Were specific products developed and used?

How were they received?

A possible way to answer those questions: use a monitoring system that tracks attendance, as well as member surveys.

Better Understanding Your Outcomes

Assessing your outcomes enables you to better know whether the programs and services you are offering are effective in helping you achieve your ultimate goal. Outcomes are the changes in beliefs, attitudes, knowledge, or action that the program produces. Were participants' skills increased or behavior modified? Were community conditions improved?

Here is a tip for developing outcome questions. First, don't start by thinking about what can be measured. Not everything that you want to achieve in your program will be measurable. Instead, think about various stakeholders and about what you want to see change over time.

Refer back to the "condition" that you want to change.

Impact on participants: How much and what kind of a difference has the program or initiative made for its targets of change? Possible questions:

How has behavior changed as a result of participation in the program?

Are participants satisfied with the experience?

Were there any negative results from participation in the program?

A possible way to answer those questions: use member surveys, interviews, and focus groups with key participants; observe at beginning and at end of work period.

Impact on the community: How much and what kind of a difference has the program or initiative made on the community as a whole? Possible questions:

What resulted from the program?

Were there any negative results from the program?

Do the benefits of the program outweigh the costs?

Possible ways to answer those questions: Conduct surveys, use interviews with key informants.

Sustaining Your Organization

A program that is ineffectual, vague, or 100 percent "invented as we go along" is not likely to be able to sustain outside funding or internal support for long. There is certainly room for invention, as there is also room for spontaneity and the crafting of a new strategy in response to an unexpected force or opportunity. But even within those realities, your organization's essential approach and the parameters it sets for its work should be within goals you've established by board and staff consensus and shaped by what you've learned through evaluation.

For the West Coast Network of Global Givers, a question that focuses on sustainability might be: "We've assumed that donors to global issues are isolated and therefore want to be organized into a network; how can we better determine what our core constituency really wants, so that we know how to proceed as an organization?"

If a similar organization recently launched in the same area with massive funding, a question to consider might be: "Is there still a need for what we're doing, in the way we are doing it? How can we test whether the need has changed, or whether there might be an additional way to meet the need?"

ASSESSING YOUR STAGE OF GROWTH: ONE ORGANIZATION'S STORY

Your organization's resources and experience will affect the evaluation approach you choose. Understanding your organizational stage of development will prepare you to select evaluation questions and information-gathering methods that best meet your current needs.

For example, the West Coast Network of Global Givers (WCNGG) began as a small organization based in Los Angeles. After having some success in organizing donors in that city, as well as increasing the amount of money they were donating to global causes, the organization decided to create "sister" networks in three additional West Coast towns. In the first year of the expansion, a lot of time was spent documenting the process of expansion. How were the three towns selected? What types of outreach efforts seemed most successful? How and for what reasons did donors in these towns come together?

Three years into the expansion effort, the evaluation questions changed substantially. In the first town, Santa Rosa, a large number of donors came together because of their frustration with immigration policy. As the first town to start a sister network, WCNGG staff spent an inordinate amount of time staffing the network and traveling back and forth between sites. The plan for the coming year was for WCNGG to shift ownership to local leadership.

In the second town, Ventura, a small group of global donors had high visibility in the community, but the organization was having trouble getting other donors interested in giving to global issues. They decided to create a pooled fund of money to support global causes and announced they would match any new network members' contribution two-to-one as a way of enticing membership and meeting their philanthropic goals.

In the third city, Sacramento, WCNGG realized it didn't have the manpower to provide intensive staffing to launch new networks. Rather, here it found a lead organization and offered to provide relevant information about global issues to interested donors.

In this second stage of evaluation, WCNGG wants to know how each of the towns meets the challenge it faces to developing a network, whether or not the networks can sustain themselves over time, and what lessons it might draw from the three towns as they develop plans for creating even more networks.

ASK WHAT YOU REALLY WANT TO KNOW

There are lots of questions you could ask that will net you information that would undoubtedly be helpful. But what do you really want to know? How can you formulate the one or two questions that will really make your evaluation both revelatory and useful?

Begin by making the following decisions:

1. Do we want to evaluate a particular program, or an aspect of the organization, or its mission as a whole?

2. If evaluating a program, what are the top two high-priority desires for that program? If evaluating an aspect of the organization, what in your current phase of development and operations are two high-priority issues?

3. If we want to look at what *we* do, that is, examine our process, do we want to look at (1) what we're offering, (2) how we're delivering it, or (3) how we can best sustain it and expand its success?

4. If we want to look at what *they* do, that is, examine our impact, what changes or actions do we hope will occur? How can we better determine how our work affects what our audience does or thinks or gains from us?

Use the sample agenda at the end of this chapter to host a meeting designed to help your leadership determine the organization's evaluation priorities for this cycle. Exhibit 4.1 provides an example of how Democracy Begins Here develops its evaluation questions and information-collection methods based on its goals.

HOW ADVOCACY ORGANIZATIONS CAN APPROACH EVALUATION

Deborah L. Puntenney (2002) says that, "Large-scale social change is almost always a grindingly slow process; success is mostly achieved in small increments, on convoluted pathways, subject to all kinds of positive and negative influences over time" (p. 6).

```
┌─────────────────────────────────────────────────────────────┐
│                          Exhibit 4.1                          │
│                  Sample Evaluation Questions                  │
│  ─────────────────────────────────────────────────────────   │
│                                                               │
│                    DEMOCRACY BEGINS HERE                      │
│                    ─────────────────                          │
│                                                               │
│          Priority Area: Teacher Professional Development      │
│                                                               │
│  *Project Goal/Desired Outcome:* Changes in instructional     │
│  practices by school teachers who participated in a           │
│  Democracy Begins Here professional development program.      │
│                                                               │
│  *Evaluation Questions:* Did faculty who experienced the      │
│  professional development change their instructional          │
│  practices? Did this vary by teachers' or by students'        │
│  characteristics? Did faculty members use the information     │
│  regarding new standards, materials, and practices? What      │
│  obstacles prevented implementing changes? What factors       │
│  facilitated change?                                          │
│                                                               │
│  *Sources of Information:* Participants, classroom observers, │
│  department chair                                             │
│                                                               │
│  *Data-Collection Methods:* Focus group with participants,    │
│  reports of classroom observers, interview with department    │
│  chair or principal                                           │
│                                                               │
└─────────────────────────────────────────────────────────────┘
```

Throughout the United States, social justice advocates are working in the nonprofit sector to advance social, economic, and cultural rights. They labor under the same financial pressures as do all nonprofits, perhaps under even greater scrutiny. Their work may be political in nature and, therefore, subject to attack from individuals and institutions with opposing points of view. They "fall outside the guidelines" for many foundations and are less likely to appeal as broadly to individual donors as social service agencies addressing basic human needs such as for food and shelter.

Small and grassroots advocacy organizations need to make the case for support as much, if not more so, than other agencies, and to do so, they need to invest in evaluation. But how do organizations "on a mission" *and* on a shoestring budget apply evaluation principles to their unique and often hard-to-quantify work?

Without the benefit of history, it is difficult if not impossible to prove how any single organization influenced events or institutions in ways that fundamentally changed the world, despite the fact that for many organizations, the mission is no less than that.

So how do you measure progress on such enormous agendas? How do you with any confidence report short-term outcomes in movements that are, by definition, long term?

For social change movements to succeed, there must be organization, that is, well-thought-out ideas with strategies and resources and numbers behind them. It is this aspect of advocacy and community-based work that evaluation can address, even if the larger questions, "Did we change public opinion?" or "Did we rewrite history?" may be impossible to answer during your tenure at the organization.

Do not assume that because your work is urgent or even sacred, you do not need to provide evidence of competence or effectiveness. You do.

If your organization is an advocacy, community organizing, or rights-focused group, your work can still be evaluated, if not on the world stage, certainly on the organizational level. As a starting point, ask what you would need to know in order to answer the following core questions:

What does your organization do for its constituents—for the population it set out to serve? Does the organization contribute to changing individual lives, policies, programs, or institutions? How?

What does your organization do for other nonprofits in its particular field? How does it influence standards or practices relative to its area of expertise and service? Does the organization add to what is already known about how to address the problem it is attempting to tackle? Is it creating models that others are following?

What does your organization do for the community at large? How has it influenced perceptions of the issues on which it works? How does it influence action on its issue?

As you think about the mind-set concerning evaluation in your organization, consider the ways you can help the board and staff move away from the perception that their work is too important to stop and evaluate; instead, help everyone understand that your work is too important not to evaluate.

As mentioned earlier, developing "the product" is only half the battle; finding the means of distribution is the other half. For smaller organizations passionate about their product, that is, their overriding mission or political agenda, the most useful focus of evaluation might not be about whether the program or mission is "good" but about how you can deliver it more effectively.

HOW TO BE ANSWERABLE WHEN ADVOCACY AND ORGANIZING ARE YOUR AGENDA

The work of grassroots and small advocacy organizations often involves the work of identifying or framing an issue, developing leaders around it, and building a constituency. If your organization is engaged in work of this nature, what sorts of questions are you asking in order to better determine your reach and impact? The questions you will need to ask and the measures you put in place to gather helpful information will be different from the kinds of questions a social service agency may ask. One way to think about all this is to focus on *capturing the benefits* of what you do rather than tracking the change that happens.

A number of models have been developed in the past few years to help social-change grantmakers better measure the impact of social-change grants. The ideas put forth in some of these models are as useful to social-change organizations as they are to grantmakers.

For example, the Women's Funding Network created an interactive online tool called "Making the Case" to help its members understand and measure social-change impact.

"Making the Case" notes that social change is complex, typically very slow, occasionally abrupt, and often nonlinear in its progression. Results can occur on multiple levels, and reflect the five indicators of social change. For grassroots organizations, these indicators provide an opportunity for reflection and suggest a set of questions that could be developed and asked.

FIVE INDICATORS OF SOCIAL CHANGE

A Shift in Definitions: Is the issue defined differently in the community or larger society?

A Shift in Behavior: Are people behaving differently in the community or larger society?

A Shift in Engagement: Are people in the community or larger society more engaged; has a critical mass of involved people been reached?

A Shift in Policy: Has an institutional, organizational, or legislative policy or practice changed?

Maintaining Past Gains: Have past gains been maintained, generally in the face of opposition?

Your organization may concentrate its work in three or four of these areas, or only one or two. Wherever you concentrate your organizational energies, that is where you should focus your evaluation questions. If your organization is in the stage of development wherein a primary component of its work is "defining the issue"—say, for example, why same-sex marriage should be legal—then it makes sense to ask how you are tackling that work and what success you are having, rather than to count the number of people who have signed on to a position statement.

Determining what your questions ought to be is the basis for planning or designing your evaluation. Everything flows from the questions your organization agrees to ask at this first stage of the process. Evaluation should address simple questions that are important to your community, your staff, and your funding partners.

DEVELOPING SPECIFIC EVALUATION QUESTIONS

Your Evaluation Questions Should be SMART:

Specific

Measurable

Action-oriented

Realistic

Timed

Source: W. K. Kellogg Foundation Logic Model Development Guide, 2004.

IDEAS FOR MEASURING ORGANIZING EFFORTS

Think about how you might develop creative ways to assess your organization's ability to do the following:

- Enable community residents to access new resources, gain new understanding of their interests, and gain new capacity to use their resources on behalf of their interests

- Identify, recruit, and develop leadership

- Broaden and deepen relationships in a community in a way that provides a foundation for action

- Tell a story about who the community network is, how it connects to the rest of the world, where it's been, and where it's going

- Provide services or advocacy generated on behalf of community interests

- Test implementation of a campaign against its original goals and deadlines

- Determine the process of the campaign: how people were recruited, battles fought, and organizations built through campaigns. Did it polarize in a way contrary to the interests of the organizing constituency, or did it unite?

- Learn how the organization balanced the work of a special campaign with the ongoing work of organization

Note: This list was adapted from Ganz, 1996.

SUPPORTING STEPS FOR ASKING THE RIGHT QUESTIONS

- ☐ At your last meeting, you clarified your organizational goals and brainstormed a list of general questions about your work or programs that evaluation would help you to answer.

- ☐ Use the following sample agendas now to help create the short list of the one or two questions you might want to address this year and the following year as part of your rolling evaluation plan.

- ☐ Begin to think about what kinds of information to track that will tell you what you need to know.

Meeting Agenda 4
Determining Evaluation Questions

1. REVIEW We have moved from identifying mission to priorities for the coming period to brainstorming questions we'd like to explore about our work and its results.

2. DISCUSS Working from the master "wish list" of possible evaluation questions that we created last time, we now need to zero in on priority questions. To more easily work through the list, go through quickly first and rank each: "S" for something we could see evaluating *sooner*, "L" for something we'd be in a better position to evaluate *later*. We need to choose from the list of questions generated last meeting the first two or three we will tackle.

3. DECIDE Which evaluation questions do we want to consider actually tackling at this time? What did we evaluate last time? Were any follow-up questions suggested? Using the rolling evaluation approach, which area do we want to spend time exploring and evaluating *this year?* What are the questions about our work that we most need to explore during this time period? Why?

From the "program" point of view, what do we most need to tackle?

From the fundraisers' point of view, what are the questions we are repeatedly asked by funders and supporters?

From the planners' point of view, what would help us prepare for the next phase of our development?

Meeting Agenda 4
Determining Evaluation Questions, Cont'd

What special considerations are there, if any? Are there more opportunities for us in some, as opposed to others? What might be on our evaluation calendar for the following year?

4. NEXT STEPS Determine cost, time line, and plan. As we move ahead, we'll use the Planning Worksheet (Worksheet 3.1) in Chapter Three to summarize our evaluation goals, methods of gathering information, time line, and evaluation budget for each year. File away the full list of possible evaluation questions created and consult it at the start of the next evaluation cycle.

Tracking Information

*Y*ou've worked with your leadership team to determine the areas of greatest priority for evaluation. You've agreed on the question or questions you want to explore during this next evaluation cycle. Now you need to track the information that will help you answer the questions you've laid out. This chapter outlines information-gathering methods and provides tools to help you do so.

OPTIONS FOR TRACKING INFORMATION

As short as it is, the word *data* can be intimidating. It suggests systems and software, experts and analysts, university advisers and scientific rigor. Not that there's anything wrong with a little scientific rigor, but being rigorous about your evaluation does not assume you must take steps beyond what your capacity allows. Evaluations can be thoughtful at any scale, just as organizations can be effective at any size.

For the purposes of evaluation, the word *data* simply means the information you have or can gather about your work, whatever that information may be. Data can include the opinions of visitors or participants, a summary of records, or trends observed. Data can be gathered from many different sources: from board and staff, community partners, or the client population you serve.

Although there are many variations on the basic options for tracking what you do, the five primary strategies listed next are really what all evaluations follow, one way or another, whether you're spending $3,000 or $3 million. You can track what you do by

1. Counting (for example, the number of attendees or participants)
2. Observing (visiting, watching, documenting)

3. Conducting interviews, focus groups, or debriefings (having one-on-one conversations with key stakeholders or facilitated conversations with small groups)

4. Conducting surveys (using information requested via mailings, forms, or phone calls)

5. Reviewing agency records (looking at reports, statistics, minutes)

How far you go with any one of these methods depends on your capacity, your budget, and what you're trying to learn. You are never "too small" to evaluate what you're doing. You can use these five basic information collection options to gather information that records your experience, no matter how small your organization.

One organization that we know of, for example, manages community gardens in neighborhoods across Chicago. The gardens themselves are usually run by only a handful of volunteers. The organization suggests that no matter what the scale of the project, at one or two meetings a year leaders and volunteers identify and reflect on the things learned during the year about managing a community garden. A volunteer can lead the discussion, and the community gardeners can then capture highlights and lowlights, triumphs and challenges. They can keep the information on file for the next wave of volunteer leaders and can send copies of their summaries to the downtown headquarters so that a composite picture of gardeners' experiences is formed.

Information gathered even in this simple way can be useful, particularly if it is collected year-to-year and organized in a thoughtful way. (See "Organizing Your Information" in Exhibit 5.1.)

Data-Collection Methods

Many newer or smaller organizations mistakenly believe that "measuring" requires developing a complex set of metrics or making use of concepts from a college statistics class. Any kind of systematic tracking counts as data collection—from a tally sheet tacked on a bulletin board to a simple spreadsheet or a customized database.

Tracking what you do is the process of refining and making more systematic some steps you're probably already taking:

1. Observing: What do observers see when they watch your program in action? What is the climate? What is the interpersonal dynamic? How prepared is the staff person to address unanticipated issues that arise?

Exhibit 5.1
Organizing Your Information

Organizing the information you collect makes it easier to see patterns and themes and to interpret meanings. You can make sense of your information through these steps:

Organize information, by

Taking notes on observations

Writing up interviews

Summarizing responses to questions

Sorting data into categories

Drawing a table or making a chart

Analyze information, by asking

What stands out?

What are the patterns?

What are the similarities?

What are the differences?

Is more information needed?

Interpret information, by asking

Do the activities accomplish their purpose?

What are the effects and outcomes?

Which findings are significant?

Which lessons can be learned?

What is to be done?

Source: Checkoway and Richards-Schuster, 2005, p. 37.

2. Conducting interviews and focus groups: What do they think about what you do? What are the commonalities and differences in their experience of your work? What insights can you garner about where you are and where you should be headed?

3. Debriefing: How did the meeting go? What did participants have to say afterwards?

4. Conducting surveys: Why are they attending, visiting, seeking services? Broadly, how satisfied are they with your work?

5. Record keeping: Who's attending, visiting, and seeking services? How far do they travel to come here? What is their demographic profile? Are there populations you hoped to reach that you are not?

6. Reviewing materials and procedures: Does the way you do it make sense, given your staffing, your constituents' needs, your funding? How are others doing it? What can you learn by looking at other organizations' approaches?

Deciding Which Data-Collection Method to Use

For each evaluation question you want to answer, consider the following:

- What information do you need to answer the question and from whom will you get it? Who do you trust to give you the information you need? Who will you believe?

- How many people (or other data sources) do you need to answer this question and believe the answers you get?

- When do you need to collect the information?

- Who will conduct the data collection?

Deciding Who Your Stakeholders Are

Think about who you want to get your information from:

- The people you are currently serving

- The people you could be serving, but aren't yet reaching

- Your program partners

- Community groups

- Grantmakers and donors

- University-based researchers, "experts" in your field, opinion-shapers

- Nonprofit leaders from organizations similar to yours

- Staff and board, volunteers, and others familiar with the internal workings of the organization

For an overview of collection methods, see Table 5.1.

Deciding About the Short Term and the Long Term

There are two basic questions for you to discuss with your team: (1) What do we need to keep track of *in general* on a regular basis, regardless of when or how we might use the information or records we want to keep? (2) What do we need to track *specifically* in order to enable us to answer the big evaluation question or questions we've identified?

In some cases, this information will be the same. In other cases, there may be a very particular kind of information that is pertinent for a limited time because of a special grant or a special situation. For example, at East Morgan Neighborhood Network, the leadership team decided to track *on a regular basis* the names and contact information of every parent who participates in any of the program's meetings, workshops, or events. In addition, because of a special two-year grant they received in response to a widely reported bullying incident at their local school, the team decided to track, *for a limited time,* the reported incidents of bullying in all area schools to determine whether the number of incidents decreased in the schools participating in the special grant initiative.

THE RIGHT GOAL STATEMENT HELPS DETERMINE THE RIGHT THINGS TO TRACK

What you measure depends on what you're trying to achieve, and you must state that desired outcome very clearly. You are not doing yourselves any favors if the desired outcome you state is impossible to achieve via your program, or impossible to measure or claim.

Imagine that the *if-then* statement you came up with earlier in your evaluation planning is, for example, "*If* we teach problem solving, peer mediation, and

Table 5.1
Overview of Methods to Collect Information

The following table provides an overview of the major methods used for collecting data during evaluations.

Method	Overall Purpose	Advantages	Challenges
Questionnaires, surveys, checklists	To quickly or easily get lots of information from people in a nonthreatening way	Can complete anonymously Inexpensive to administer Easy to compare and analyze Can be administered to many people Can get lots of data Many sample questionnaires already exist	Might not get careful feedback Wording can bias client's responses Are impersonal In surveys, may need sampling expert Doesn't get full story
Interviews	To fully understand someone's impressions or experiences or learn more about his or her answers to questionnaires	Get full range and depth of information Develops relationship with client Can be flexible with client	Can take much time Can be hard to analyze and compare Can be costly Interviewer can bias client's responses
Documentation review	To gain impression of how program operates without interrupting the program; comes from review of applications, finances, memos, minutes, and so on	Get comprehensive and historical information Doesn't interrupt program or client's routine in program Information already exists Few biases about information	Often takes much time Information may be incomplete Need to be quite clear about what's being looked for Not flexible means to get data; data restricted to what already exists

Method	Overall Purpose	Advantages	Challenges
Observation	To gather accurate information about how a program actually operates, particularly about processes	View operations of a program as they are actually occurring; Can adapt to events as they occur	Can be difficult to interpret behaviors, as observed; Can be complex to categorize observations; Can influence behaviors of program participants; Can be expensive
Focus groups	To explore a topic in depth through group discussion, for example, about reactions to an experience or suggestion, understanding common complaints; useful in evaluation and marketing	Quickly and reliably get common impressions; Can be efficient way to get much range and depth of information in short time; Can convey key information about programs	Can be hard to analyze responses; Need good facilitator for safety and closure; Difficult to schedule 6–8 people together
Case studies	To fully understand or depict client's experiences in a program and conduct comprehensive examination through cross-comparison of cases	Fully depicts client's experience in program input, process, and results; Powerful means to portray program to outsiders	Usually quite time-consuming to collect, organize, and describe; Represents depth of information, rather than breadth

Source: McNamara, 1998.

conflict resolution skills in the middle school, *then* we will create a stronger ethic of nonviolence at our school, and there will be fewer incidents of bullying." If you were evaluating the first part of that statement—your services—you might want to track how many teachers get training and how they incorporate what they learn into the school day. If you were evaluating the second part of that statement—your outcomes—then you might want to track how many times incidents occur or create a system for rewarding students who are peacemakers.

Tracking the Right Thing

Although all nonprofits want to be ambitious, it is also important to be realistic. Sometimes work done by a single organization has its greatest impact by virtue of being part of a larger movement, which can make "results" in a short time difficult to pinpoint. The task becomes easier, however, if the desired outcome you identify is focused tightly on your work, even if the impact you desire relates to large community or social change.

The West Coast Global Donors Network, for example, seeks to "promote, encourage and support California-based donors in their international giving in order to increase the amount and impact of international philanthropy." What is the ultimate impact they seek? More dollars going to global causes. But given their mission statement, is there a more immediate outcome they can measure—an outcome closer at hand and more directly related to their own work with members?

- What they do: "promote, encourage and support donors on the west coast in their international giving"
- What they hope others will do: "increase the amount and quality of international giving and generate support for global issues within philanthropy"
- How they can evaluate what they do:

  Examine the group: How many donors became members or supporters of the network; are there more members than there were a year ago; and did the people who came to their program and events represent the people they wanted to reach?

  Examine the services: Did what they offered through the Network actually encourage and support their members? How do they know that?

What about what others do? Can they evaluate whether or not their work increased the amount and impact of international philanthropy? Not easily. They might look at the *amount* of giving by members, and ask members about the extent to which the Network was a factor in influencing their giving. But it would be hard to isolate, in many instances, whether or not increased donations came about because of the Network's influence as opposed to, say, the death of a wealthy relative or a new international business interest.

Questions they might legitimately ask in the process of an evaluation, however, might instead address matters such as these:

> Have we, in fact, promoted, encouraged, and supported West Coast–based donors? Did we do it well? How do we know we did it well?

> If we call ourselves a network, what does it mean for us to be powerful as a network? What are the key characteristics of a powerful and successful donor network? How closely do we match that ideal?

Tracking What *You* Do (Process)

Looking at what you do tends to focus on the activities you engage in, the services you provide, the effectiveness of the strategies you are using, whether you are meeting the goals you've set, and whether the stakeholders you intend to reach through your work think you are useful.

Tracking what *you* do typically involves reviewing your own internal records, gathering feedback from staff and key volunteers, looking at how what you do stacks up against current best practices or standards in your field, and, of course, comparing what you're doing to what you said was your goal.

But what about *results?* How does counting the meetings you've hosted, the exhibits you've presented, and the rallies you've organized speak to the outcomes you hope to achieve? Before you can assess the kind of impact you've had, you've got to know whether the training was actually implemented as planned, or the curriculum you developed was used, or the play was produced as envisioned. Sometimes a desired outcome does not occur because the program couldn't be implemented. Sometimes it doesn't occur because the program doesn't achieve the expected results.

Tracking What *They* Do as a Result (Outcome)

In the largest sense, the results you are trying to achieve relate to what *they* do—to the behaviors you want to be able to claim are changing because of your work. How does measuring and describing the shifting dimensions of the group you are serving speak to results?

Looking at what *they* do tends to focus not so much on services as on the group or population—in other words, on your members, your clients, your audience, or the legislators. Looking at what *they* do tends to involve asking questions that help you determine whether that group is growing or shrinking, progressing or declining, succeeding or failing, acting or remaining passive, changing or remaining the same, responding to you or ignoring you.

Tracking what *they* do typically involves participant interviews surveys, observation, and the regular tracking of events, actions, and developments related to the area you're trying to influence.

Challenges Involved in Tracking Long-Term Impact

Where does impact come from? It comes from multiple outcomes over time. The work you do—the process you engage in—results in multiple outcomes. For example, a campaign to reduce lead poisoning might include producing a newsletter, holding a community rally, and airing targeted public service announcements. The outcomes of these activities may include such developments as these: ten legislators agree to meet with your leaders, five school principals take the issue to their PTOs, and six child care centers launch lead-abatement programs. The ultimate *impact* may be the reduction of lead poisoning in children in your area, which other organizations may also contribute to achieving.

Because impact is the result of multiple outcomes over time, it can be difficult to cite at year's end in an annual report, and it is unrealistic to assume that you should be able to do so.

You can gather *some* information about whether or not the behaviors you are hoping to change are indeed changing, and you can *sometimes* claim that some of that is because of your work. However, for small-budget organizations, there are very real limitations. Even in the best-case scenario, the information you might successfully consolidate will more likely resemble "circumstantial evidence" than hard proof.

Effective nonprofits can track the results of their efforts in general and report back to supporters consistently. Whether that tracking takes on the form of statistical evidence constitutes a complicated question. Nonprofits, especially large ones, can and do partner with research organizations to track the success of program graduates five years after completing the program, host focus groups with visitors or patrons, and conduct surveys that gather information about large populations served. Gathering and interpreting quantifiable results presents a number of challenges for smaller organizations and may not be that useful to the organization in the end.

Conducting research on program impact requires large outlays of resources. A small program working on fostering self-esteem among teen girls, for example, may not have the money, staff, or expertise to conduct a multiyear, longitudinal study that determines how many girls remained drug-free five years after leaving the program, much less how the program changed the entire community.

Such an organization can, however, gather information about the program in other ways: reports on the number of girls served, examples of activities they undertook, descriptions of participant interactions with other programs or the surrounding community, interviews with the girls themselves. Moreover, since the goal of evaluation is to improve your work as much as it is to prove or document it, allowing the "interpretive task" to take place around the staff or board table, rather than through sophisticated academic or computer analysis, ensures that stakeholders will engage with and learn from findings.

In many cases, a program's larger societal impact is difficult to track, especially in the short term. A group working to end police brutality is probably not going to accomplish that in one or two years. A health risk-reduction program may be able to report how many people attended its play about AIDS, but can it quantify how the play affected the people who saw it, how many adopted safe sex practices as a result, or how many friends they talked to about it afterwards?

Sometimes we simply can't isolate our good work from the good work of our colleagues; we work together to make change, and over time, with constant pressure and attention, change occurs. For example, if there are twenty-three special programs at work in a public school, and each one is aimed at improving test scores, which program in the end can claim responsibility for an increase in test scores that ends up occurring three years later? And how does the radically changing demographic of the neighborhood in which test scores rose affect the validity of that program's claim? What about the fact that a weak principal left and a terrific one came in during the same time period?

Helpful Hints: Developing Survey, Focus Group, and Individual Interview Questions:

- Develop questions that give people a point of reference:

  Compared to other programs

  Compared to your expectation

  Compared to other trainings you've attended

  Compared to what you understood when you joined the program

- Reduce the tendency to rate a program highly by asking focused questions in which people can identify something that can be improved:

  What did the instructor do well?

  What can the instructor do better next time?

  What did you find most helpful?

  What did you find not so helpful?

  How can the program be improved?

- Prepare your system to analyze the data so that you are sure you can use what you gather. For example, surveys are intended to reach a broad scope of people but hard to analyze and tabulate if you have too many open-ended questions. In focus groups, limit the number of questions to ten to twelve so that everyone has the opportunity to talk.

- Plan to ask roughly the same set of questions to each person you interview so that you can more easily compare responses later. For guidelines on how to word your questions, as well as examples of questions, see Exhibits 5.2 and 5.3.

Exhibit 5.2
Guidelines on Wording Questions

Refer to one thing at a time. Asking clients whether the service facility they visited was "safe and clean" does not allow for determining whether a "no" answer refers to safety, cleanliness, or both.

Choose terms clients can understand. Asking whether clients are substance abuse "recidivists," for example, may be beyond the comprehension of some.

Eliminate negative questions. Questions should not require a client to respond "yes" in order to mean "no." For example, the question, "Was the service not provided in a timely manner?" is difficult to understand. The answer is equally difficult to interpret.

Avoid leading or biased questions. Asking, "Isn't the new collection of books in the library much better than the old collection?" invites a "yes" answer, as opposed to a more neutral version: "Would you say the current collection of books is better or worse than the previous collection?" Another option, although longer, is, "Some library clients believe that the current collection of books is better than the previous collection. Others believe that the previous collection was better than the current collection. What do you think?"

Provide appropriate and reasonable time references. Make clear which time period is being asked about, but avoid asking clients to recall events that occurred a long time ago. For example, when asking about the promptness of ride-on transportation, it is appropriate to specify a time period, but asking whether service was generally on time a year ago is unlikely to produce a reliable answer.

Make questions consistent if comparisons over time or across groups are to be made from survey to survey. Even if previously used wording is not ideal, word-for-word consistency is important to ensure that comparisons are valid.

Source: Adapted from Abravanel, 2003.

Exhibit 5.3
One Group's Questions

WHAT WE LEARNED ABOUT MANAGING A COMMUNITY GARDEN

Welcome to Our Annual Learning and Sharing Meeting!

Thank you so much for coming. Our discussions are always fun and informative; they help us record our history and prepare for next year. We want to get your feedback on many questions, but most important, ask you what are the *two or three most important things you learned this year.* Today, our discussion will be led by

_____ .

Why you are involved in community gardening

1. What drew you to this project and keeps you active in it?
2. How easy or difficult is it to define your garden's mission/goals?
3. How easy or difficult has it been to get support from your group?
4. To what extent do you feel your community garden is reaching its goals?
5. What would be your advice to others about both articulating and working toward their goals for their garden?

Working as a group of volunteers to create a garden

1. How difficult or easy has it been to work as a group toward your goal?
2. What are some of the problems you face on a regular basis?
3. What have been your triumphs?
4. What advice would you give those in leadership roles at other gardens?
5. What advice would you give to volunteers regarding their relationships with their gardens' "leaders"?
6. Are there resources you wish you had that would help you in working with or leading your group?
7. What has it been like recruiting volunteers for your garden?

Working with the city

1. What kind of contact have you had with the city in relationship to the garden?
2. If there have been any problems, what could be put in place to deal with those problems in the future?

Exhibit 5.3
One Group's Questions, Cont'd

3. Do you feel you know all you need to know about city regulations and ordinances?

4. If not, in what way could we help you with this?

Day-to-day operations

1. What does it take for your garden to function well during the growing season?

2. How do you set up your schedules for watering, weeding, and so on?

3. What are your biggest obstacles to the process running smoothly?

4. What makes a high-functioning garden (for both people and plants)?

Partnerships with community

1. What are the greatest challenges of working with outside organizations (schools, arts groups, neighborhood associations, and so on)?

2. What are the benefits?

3. What makes these partnerships healthy?

4. What limits their effectiveness?

Telling your story

1. Knowing what you know now, putting yourself in the place of a new community gardener, what would be the most effective way to let them know what you know?

2. Which stories of your garden absolutely need to be told to others embarking on the same path?

3. What has been your low point/high point in this journey?

4. What makes it all worthwhile?

5. What are the two or three most important things you learned this year?

6. How would you feel about keeping a written and/or photographic journal of your garden and its progress?

7. What could we provide you with that would make this task easier?

Source: Atkinson and Philbin, 2006. Available through Neighbor Space, 25 East Washington, Suite 1670, Chicago IL 60602.

SUPPORTING STEPS FOR TRACKING INFORMATION

☐ You've established goals or desired outcomes for each of your priority areas or programs. You can state the goal in a sentence or two. As suggested in the "Quick Exercise" (Exhibit 2.3), now ask yourselves what the key *indicators* might be that would provide evidence that those goals are being met. Do you already have systems in place to keep track of those things, to collect that information?

☐ Use the sample meeting agenda at the end of this chapter to review the questions you've chosen to explore for your evaluation and determine what measures you can track that will help you get the information you need.

☐ Determine with your team the easiest ways to collect the information you've now decided you want to collect. For example, if a good information source for determining annual participation in your community meeting is the meeting sign-in sheets, who will collect them each month? Will they be put in a file folder or entered into a computer database? How will you tabulate them?

☐ If you are going to survey or interview stakeholders, gather your team to think about and write down the questions you want to ask. Test these questions on a small group of "critical friends" or insiders first.

☐ Consider instituting an annual "information-gathering meeting"—a regular year-end meeting at which you thank your volunteers, members, or program participants and gather opinions and capture stories. Not only will you have a record of your year, but after a few years, you'll be able to see trends and patterns. Go back over the sample set of questions in Exhibit 5.3 and adapt those for your own organization.

Meeting Agenda 5
Choosing Indicators

How We'll Measure Our Progress

1. REVIEW Check in on our last meeting. Summarize the two or three big questions we agreed that this evaluation will address.

Check our choices against these evaluation standards:

Is the question we chose *useful*?

Is it *feasible* for us to gain information in that area and evaluate in the way we'd like?

Is it *appropriate* given our mission, values, the population we serve?

Have we laid out the question in a way that will enable us to be *accurate* as we collect data and draw conclusions?

2. DISCUSS What would success look like for us in each of these areas?

3. DECIDE Look at the examples of "what success would look like" that we just generated. How could we translate these indications of progress into steps we could actually measure?

4. NEXT STEPS Come to the next meeting with suggestions as to what we'll need in order to gather the kind of information we described. How will we track this information? So that we are better prepared for next year, of all that we could track, what should we track on a regular, ongoing basis? What will be particularly important for us to compare *year-to-year*?

5. NEXT MEETING Report on any challenges or new considerations regarding the gathering of information.

Note: Standards are based on Sanders, 1994.

Learning From and Using the Information

*O*nce you have gathered your information, it's time to analyze it and draw some conclusions. This will involve examining the findings for patterns or discrepancies, interpreting what they mean, and identifying follow-up actions to consider as a result of the evaluation findings.

MAKING USE OF YOUR INFORMATION

Does data speak for itself? Sometimes, but not often enough. The truth is that data is always subject to interpretation. A special event that nets $75,000 may seem like a success on the surface, but perhaps it would seem less so if you learn that it required seven hundred staff hours to pull off. Even knowing that it consumed that much staff time, one board member might conclude that the event was still worth it while another might decide the payoff is not worth the staff time involved. Without considering the data against the goals that you set and the questions you wanted answered, it would be difficult to determine which board member's perspective made the most sense for the organization.

Where evaluation is concerned, the interpretive tasks at the end of the process are where all the learning comes and where making real use of the evaluation begins. As you begin the interpretive process, keep in mind that analyzing and drawing conclusions—even with the best possible data at your fingertips—is a subjective process. The conclusions that one set of leaders draw one year (or in one meeting) will not necessarily be the same as the conclusions another set of

91

leaders draw. This is one of the primary reasons that setting clear goals for each activity or program in advance is essential; it is much easier to determine whether or not you got to the right spot if, before setting out, everyone agreed exactly on where they wanted to go.

ORGANIZING YOUR INFORMATION

Keep your evaluation goal in mind as you go over your information. Doing so will help ensure that you stay focused on the questions you sought to answer at the beginning of your evaluation process. For example, if you sought to learn how your organization's members perceive your work, you might simply organize your information into three categories: strengths, weaknesses, and suggestions for the future. If you sought to learn more about the outcome of a particular campaign or advocacy effort, you would organize your data in a way that allowed you to see where progress was made and where progress was stalled.

You can break down or group pieces of information in whatever manner makes most sense for answering your evaluation question. For example, as illustrated in Table 6.1, you may want to sort the opinions you gathered according to the type of person from whom you sought opinions: "this is what people who attended programs in the evening tended to say" or "this is how senior citizens involved in our community gardening project responded." The same table can also be adapted to use with focus-group findings and document review.

This kind of chart provides an at-a-glance summary of different stakeholder perceptions, which makes it easier to share with board members and other readers than the full report. However, especially for internal review, you would also want to keep on file a complete summary of interviews, including some exact quotes from participants that illustrate particularly important points, as well as more discussion of the views that were shared and their meaning for your work.

DRAWING CONCLUSIONS

Evaluation is one part art and one part science, and it can take some time to figure out the right information to track and analyze. At times you will not understand or like your findings because you chose the wrong (inadequate, inaccurate, and so on) thing to track and measure; this does not mean you failed. On the contrary, it means you succeeded in launching an evaluation program. Second, unlike statistical research methods, the interpretive task is done with real people and not

Table 6.1
Sample Summary of Interviews

Interview Question	Interview Respondents' Comments			
	Funders	Collaborative Partners	Organization Members	Community Institutions
From your standpoint, what was the organization's most significant accomplishment last year?	75 percent said recruiting community members to school board seats.	Nearly 100 percent said our outreach to identify new community members and engage them in our work.	Half said most important was our convening them monthly, handling logistics.	60 percent said our presence in the neighborhood; 30 percent said our training programs; 10 percent didn't know us well enough to comment.

with a computer program. This means that people will sometimes disagree about what the findings say and mean. *And they will all be right in their own way.* Again, this does not mean you have failed to "get it right." On the contrary. It means you have succeeded with the ultimate purpose of evaluation: to get people reflecting on and talking about the purpose of their work and what plans best support it.

Chicago-based consultant Susannah Quern Pratt suggests that organizations use a simple schematic, shown in Figure 6.1, to help them with the interpretation of their data and to identify whether or not changes need to be made to the evaluation plan for the next year.

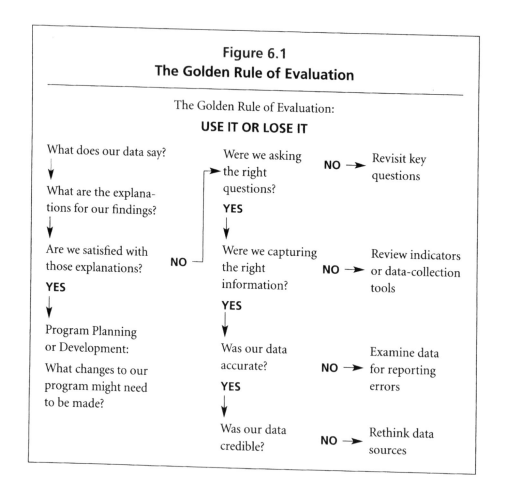

Figure 6.1
The Golden Rule of Evaluation

The Golden Rule of Evaluation:

USE IT OR LOSE IT

What does our data say?
↓
What are the explanations for our findings?
↓
Are we satisfied with those explanations?   **NO**
YES
↓
Program Planning or Development:
What changes to our program might need to be made?

Were we asking the right questions?   **NO →** Revisit key questions
YES
↓
Were we capturing the right information?   **NO →** Review indicators or data-collection tools
YES
↓
Was our data accurate?   **NO →** Examine data for reporting errors
YES
↓
Was our data credible?   **NO →** Rethink data sources

Begin by asking yourself what the information you collected suggests about your work. Is there information that is particularly surprising or significantly different from what you had expected? What is reassuring about what you learned? Begin to think about the possible explanations for your surprise. What might the information suggest that you had not considered before? Work in a team and push yourselves to make sure you consider all the possibilities. If you are satisfied with the information and its findings, then begin to develop a bullet-point list of what it suggests for areas of your work to be strengthened, highlighted, or adapted. Be sure to list both the positive findings and the negative findings as you go about listing potential ways to use the information to boost your work.

If you are not satisfied with what the information suggests, it is time to go back to the evaluation plan and revisit whether or not you were asking the right questions and gathering the right information.

In one example, a team of physicians, social workers, and lawyers provided coordinated services to low-income families with premature infants. The goal was to ensure better access to medical care and social services. Academic researchers conducted a costly scientific evaluation to see whether families in the project fared better than families who did not receive services. To everyone's great surprise, the data showed no difference between the project families and the control-group families. Yet everyone in the project team believed the research did not reflect the real-life difference that they saw their services make with patients and families on a daily basis.

The group asked themselves, did we ask the right questions? What do we know from our experience that is not reflected in our evaluation findings? Did we collect the wrong type of information? How can we explain this discrepancy?

Look to see whether you asked the types of questions that related directly to the information you sought to obtain. Or review the methods used to collect information. If you had hoped to get feedback on community priorities over the next three years and surveyed community members broadly, they might not have known enough about the work of your organization to provide meaningful feedback. Maybe surveys of those community members who are also members of your organization could be pulled out and re-interpreted. The project leaders in the example determined that they had asked the wrong question. They were able to re-sort their information to look at a different question and the results more closely mirrored what everyone in the project knew in their hearts and minds to be more reflective of their experiences.

WAYS TO ANALYZE SURVEY DATA

The way that you look at the information you gather is as important as the information itself. Here are some ways that you might consider organizing your information:

Comparisons across stakeholder subgroups. This comparison involves separating information gleaned in interviews, surveys, or focus groups, for example, by key demographic or other characteristics and comparing the results across subgroups. For example, the analysis could separate stakeholder responses by age, by the role they play, or by their level of involvement in the project. Such comparisons are likely very useful for identifying programmatic problems. Satisfaction ratings or improvement in condition may vary by stakeholder type, the amount or type of service received, the program offering the service, or who provided the service.

Comparisons against goals. This comparison shows whether the organization is meeting, exceeding, or failing to meet its goals.

Comparisons with previous surveys. This comparison allows for the analysis of trends and indicates whether outcomes are improving, worsening, or staying constant over time.

Comparisons against best practices and other standards in a particular field. Where there are appropriate external benchmarks, this type of comparison also shows how the organization's outcomes measure up.

Comparisons of responses to one question with responses to others. Cross-question comparisons help to describe patterns and explain why answers vary. For example, overall dissatisfaction with services may be highest for those clients who are dissatisfied with the accessibility of the service facility. The comparison can help identify the extent to which service quality characteristics (such as accessibility) are important to overall client satisfaction.

Source: Adapted from Abravanel, 2003, p. 33.

The point is to use and learn from the information you get. If it doesn't at first appear to reflect your experience, don't ignore it. Identify why and learn from that. Evaluation is about learning.

USING WHAT YOU LEARN

Evaluation and planning are interrelated and are part of an ongoing cycle.

The most useful evaluation is one set up to *feed directly into your planning* for next year or the next set of years. Rather than addressing an abstract set of questions that no one really knows how to make use of after the evaluation report is finished, a useful evaluation anticipates practical and urgent questions that staff and board will want to consider as they begin planning for the new year or new cycle of programming.

Depending on the area your evaluation addressed, evaluation results can be used in the longer-term process of strategic planning or in the shorter-term process of developing budgets, benchmarks, and program goals for an annual work plan. If you are making use of rolling evaluation and are evaluating only one or two specific areas per year, you may be simply linking what you learned to the benchmarks you plan to set for a particular program for the coming year. As you proceed with your rolling evaluation, tackling an ever-expanding list of related questions year-by-year, you will eventually be looking at three or four years of data as you embark on a multiyear strategic planning effort. And as your experience grows, along with your data, you will find that what you learn *over time* provides the strongest evidence of the overall impact your program is having.

Use evaluation results to

- *Make your case:* Make the case to new and old board members, individual supporters, funders, the media, other nonprofits, community leaders, skeptics and critics, and friends.

- *Plan your next move:* Now that you know something you didn't know a year ago, what would you do differently? What would you invest in more? Less?

- *Gain perspective:* Examine the assumptions you make about your work, on other programs that you may now see in a new light, or on the field in which your organization is operating.

- *Identify resources needed:* See whether you will need staff and volunteer training, technical assistance, or other resources that would help you more effectively reach your goals.

Do not use evaluation results to

- *Punish staff* (though evaluation can identify staff and management issues that need to be addressed)
- *Distract from other issues or cover up a problem*
- *Spend over your budget*
- *Overconfidently dismiss alternate views or approaches*
- *Prove to the world how good you are* (although it's good to toot your horn and show your results, don't do it at the expense of learning how to be even better)

When and Where Do We Use Our Results?

Use your evaluation results for decision making at staff and board meetings, annual and strategic planning, for budgeting, and for identifying skills needed in new hires. You can also use your results for show-and-tell moments. This includes grant reports to funders, proposals to prospective funders, and annual reports, as well as at board and community meetings, in your media communications, and as part of your public education or policy advocacy efforts.

What If You Don't Like the Results?

Sometimes the results of an evaluation can be challenging or disappointing, revealing things that stakeholders do not want to hear or know. Sometimes evaluation reveals realities that require difficult decisions (for example, letting a staff member go, or ending a program that staff is passionate about but that isn't really suited to the organization's capacities).

Confusion or disagreement as to the use of results occurs most often when evaluation results are *not* what everyone anticipated or hoped, especially in cases where the evaluation question was less a question than a statement that the organization hoped that some modest research would simply confirm. And it didn't.

If your organization began its evaluation hoping to come up with some new ways of tooting its horn, your leadership is likely to be mightily disappointed if the evaluation suggests that some program strategies are perhaps not as effective as everyone had assumed. Evaluation results may not always be easy to digest, but the information that evaluation provides enables you to make the adjustments that need to be made.

MAKING THE CASE FOR SUPPORT

One of the greatest external uses for your evaluation is in helping your organization make its case for support, which can be incorporated into proposals, put at the heart of fundraising appeals, and embedded in the language that staff and board routinely use to describe your organization's work.

Your case for support should be committed to paper and included in materials supplied to new board members and new staff. It should be reviewed regularly and updated as new and more powerful "evidence" of your impact becomes available or as new ways of making your best arguments take shape.

For example, at East Morgan Neighborhood Network project, key findings from evaluations are prominent in the organization's case for support and in its fundraising materials:

Students who participate in our after-school programs are graduating from high school at 18 percent higher rates than their peers.

Girls involved in our after-school program engaged in community service projects at twice the national average for their age group.

A "case statement" or "case for support" should generally include the following components, for which your evaluation can be one source of information:

- The need for your services

- Why you are the best organization to fulfill those needs in terms of the quality of your programming, the strength of your leadership, the management of your resources, the fulfillment of your mission

- A call to action

Sometimes we don't like the results because, in fact, we haven't captured the right information. Possibly we picked the wrong indicators or distributed the survey to the wrong group. Here are some principles to keep in mind as you ponder your evaluation results:

The evaluation process is ongoing. Evaluation often begins with high hopes and great curiosity, and sometimes ends with a fizzle as staff or board mutter that "we didn't really learn anything" or as leaders resist drawing conclusions and making changes that might signal turmoil.

Evaluation is a *process* that builds on itself and on your history and practice, and that provides information that is most useful by virtue of being cumulative. There may be some years when the results were not quite as exciting as you'd hoped, but it all goes into creating greater understanding of the progress your organization is making.

Problems will occur, of course. If you conduct evaluation over many years, you will at some point experience some of the following:

- *A flat result.* The evaluation told us what we sort of knew anyway and, as a result, it's dull.

Consolation: It's still useful information.

- *No one believes it.* It's all there in black and white, but even our own people have a hard time believing our findings.

Consolation: You now have a reason to engage in an important discussion: What assumptions did people make that now are being challenged? What issues are being raised by the findings?

- *Everything changed before we finished.* The funding was cut, the lead staff person moved to Oklahoma, and the question we set out to answer became irrelevant.

Consolation: Now you can move on the other question that was second runner-up. And consider it all part of the learning process.

- *Now we have more work to do.* The evaluation showed that what we're doing is working, but would be greatly enhanced if we added an additional component.

Consolation: There will always be more work, and at least now you have a better idea of what the work should be that is likely to net the greatest results.

- *Our board chair counters every new idea by saying, "but the evaluation said—"* Thank goodness the board read and understood the evaluation, but some board members now seem fixated on doing nothing but what the evaluation suggested, whereas staff are seeing some new creative opportunities outside the scope of the evaluation.

  Consolation: You have engaged your board in some core program work issues.

- *Picking daisies, ignoring weeds.* The evaluation raised some prickly points, and everyone is ignoring the prickliest.

  Consolation: At least the prickly points have been raised, and you can quote from the evaluation. Before, perhaps, you couldn't make the point at all. Leaders need to continually bring up the unpopular findings internally until the organization realizes these findings cannot be ignored and takes steps to address them.

- *Again? We just did an evaluation.* Didn't we learn what we needed to know last time?

  Consolation: There's always something new to learn, and if you assume evaluation is ongoing and eternal, you won't need to deal with this attitude for long. Evaluation will become a part of your annual work plan.

SHARING YOUR EVALUATION RESULTS WITH THE OUTSIDE WORLD

If you have followed the recommendations in this book, your evaluation report should provide you with useful information that illuminates your work and answers a very specific set of questions about what you're doing and how what you're doing is perceived.

However, in addition to what you intend the report to reveal, it may also reveal other factors relative to how your organization functions. Every aspect of your evaluation paints a picture of your organization: to a funder or an outsider, it may reveal the assumptions your organization makes about its issue or its territory; it may reveal an organization's level of sophistication or lack thereof; it may reveal how closely (or not) you work with your board.

Before you disseminate your evaluation report widely, ask yourself what kind of reactions or responses the findings might generate. Are there any surprises? Are there special strengths you want to underscore or weaknesses you want to acknowledge? It is valuable to cite the weaknesses along with the organization's plans for improvements and adjustments.

FEEDING RESULTS INTO THE CYCLE OF PLANNING

Evaluation is a component of an overall cycle that involves planning, implementation, evaluation, and then planning again. This cycle happens according to whatever natural timetable works for your program or organization and the specific area you are evaluating, but it also relates to that larger territory of strategic planning, which provides the "big picture" guidance, imposed over all areas.

Evaluation planning should not be left out of strategic planning (unfortunately, it often is), because useful and realistic strategic planning is dependent on thoughtful and timely use of evaluation results. The following list is a guide to strategic planning that illustrates how evaluation fits into the overall planning cycle.

A strategic plan is ultimately no more and no less than a set of decisions about what to do, why to do it, and how to do it. A strategic plan typically includes the following components:

Who We Are

- Mission statement
- Vision statement
- Statement of core values
- Primary constituents or audience
- Secondary constituents or audience

Where We Are Headed

- Key organizational goals
- Your vision for growth and development

How We Achieve

- Primary goals/summary

  Goal 1

  Rationale

  Strategy to achieve that goal

TYING EVALUATION INTO PLANNING

The uses for evaluation are both short term and long term. Nonprofit organizations can rarely synchronize all parts in perfect harmony, so there's no reason to assume that you will always be able to time the completion of your most recent evaluation to, say, the start of your budget season or the scheduling of your board retreat. To the extent possible, however, you do not want to begin planning for your next phase of development without the advantage of feedback on how things went in the last phase.

Because program calendars and timetables don't always jibe with the calendar of board meetings and budget deadlines, evaluation results are often most useful in terms of the way they help to inform the overall strategic direction in which a program or organization is heading, which makes results useful at any time, no matter when your final report is completed.

The rolling evaluation approach that this book recommends for smaller organizations is an approach that is cumulative. No single evaluation will tell you in any definitive way what you are accomplishing overall, but when looked at in clusters over time, evaluation results paint a clearer, more meaningful picture.

DECIDING WHERE TO BEGIN

As you examine evaluation results and begin planning, you should begin by asking the following three questions:

1. How successful were we in reaching the desired outcomes or goals we set in the area our evaluation tackled this year?

2. What might we do next year to improve our programs and services in this area?

3. How might these improvements lead to greater impact in the future?

Creating plans that set specific goals and that can more easily be evaluated makes both planning and evaluation easier.

INCORPORATING EVALUATION INTO YOUR STRATEGIC PLANNING PROCESS

You may or may not already have in place a process for doing strategic planning on a regular basis. If you do not have a strategic plan guiding your work at present, take the time to do one. Although some plans make projections for longer periods of time, for smaller organizations, a strategic plan covering two to three years is reasonable.

SAMPLE PROCESS:
STRATEGIC PLANNING INVOLVING VOLUNTEER LEADERSHIP

At the first stage:

- *Determine your team; commit to a process.* Will you complete your planning work in three months? Six months? Who will lead? Will your planning team include a representative from your evaluation team?

- *Inform and involve other key players in other areas or departments.* Let leaders of existing committees or projects know that you will want their involvement in a strategic planning process. What kind of participation do you envision from representatives of committees, projects, or departments? Let them know what you want them to do, in what format, by what dates.

At the second stage:

- *Review the evaluation learning and assess your program and organizational needs.* What did your last evaluation suggest you need to do in your next round of work? What are the long-term goals you hope to reach, the competency or impact your evaluations have been measuring? What are the strengths, weaknesses, needs, and opportunities overall that you might want to consider as you embark on strategic planning?

- *Identify the big questions in each key area* (program, operations, development) that you want the strategic planning process to address. (What do we want to look like "then" versus what we look like "now"? Should we use the building for. . . ? How soon could we launch a. . . ? Do we need to invest in. . . ?) A strategic plan should cover more than just "program." At its most basic, strategic planning is simply about identifying questions and then going about the process of answering them, one-by-one, with plans.

- *Plan a stakeholder or community input "sounding board" event when some trial balloons are ready to be floated.* Or you might do it as part of a buy-in and community-relations effort. What do constituents consider key questions? Is there any initial reaction to any areas or ideas you want to test?

- *Tackle the questions.* Working groups (or standing committees) or key liaisons for each area then tackle those questions, help to define the overriding goals for their area, and come up with some recommendations as to strategies that could be put in place to meet those goals. Areas covered by the plan would include evaluation. If your strategic plan is for the next three years, it should include your next three years of projected evaluation questions or topics.

At the third stage:

- *Planning team regroups to review input, ideas, and recommendations.* These will have been generated by staff leaders and committees; goals will have been defined by committees or leadership teams in each area. The planning team makes or refines recommendations based on mission fit, resources, feasibility.

- *Planning team drafts a document.* The document should include (1) key goals, (2) the rationale for each goal, (3) the strategies that will help you achieve each one. In areas where evaluation has been conducted, the goals should relate to your past evaluation findings or future evaluation calendar.

And finally:

- Submit the document to the board, and revise it after that meeting as necessary; the board ultimately approves.

- Share the plan, first with key stakeholders such as subcommittees, and then with constituents as a whole.

- Staff and volunteers implement the plan; they revisit the plan often, updating annually.

SUPPORTING STEPS FOR LEARNING AND USING

☐ Use The Golden Rule of Evaluation (shown in Figure 6.1) to help you interpret your data and identify whether or not changes need to be made to the evaluation plan for the next year.

☐ Use the following sample agenda to conduct the meetings that will help you draw conclusions from your evaluation and apply what you've learned to your plans for next year.

☐ Make sure that as you are envisioning the future for your organization and projecting the growing impact of its work, you are taking into consideration what your evaluation tells you.

Meeting Agenda 6
Learning and Using Results

1. REVIEW Summarize key findings and their implications. Review the one- or two-page bullet point highlights that staff will pass out.

2. DISCUSS Before we disseminate this evaluation report further, what do we anticipate might be the response? Are there any surprises? Are there special strengths we want to underscore, or weaknesses we want to acknowledge and plan to address?

3. DECIDE Identify any strategies or changes we should consider as we move ahead.

In what ways does what we learn have an impact on

- Our Planning

As we plan for next season, which evaluation findings are particularly important for us to keep in mind?

- Our Programming

Based on what we learned, what adjustments should we make?

- Our Fundraising and Marketing

How can we best convey evaluation findings to our funders and individual donors?

- Our Community Relations

How can we share relevant findings with our colleagues and constituents?

What events, publications, and vehicles will we use?

4. NEXT STEPS Plan for next year.

Commonly Used Terms and Their Definitions

When talking about your evaluation, it is important to make sure that everyone understands the terms being used. All too often, people use evaluation terms in different ways. It is helpful to clarify terminology at the outset.

Activities: The services a program provides. What will you do to accomplish your goals?

    Example: After-school tutoring will be provided for elementary school students, as well as parent leadership training for parents.

Benchmarks or measures: An organization's target level of performance for a particular outcome measure; quantifiable indicators that demonstrate progress toward an outcome, typically during a one-year timeframe. "How will you know you have achieved your goals?"

    Example: Students will read five new books in one semester; twenty parents will complete training.

Data: Any information you gather. The term *data* is not limited to statistics, demographics, mathematical measurements, and metrics. It might indicate notes based on the observations of program activities. "What information will you collect in order to determine if you achieved your benchmark or goal?"

    Example: Tutors and students working together will be observed; intake questionnaire will be given to parents participating in leadership training.

Impact: The long-term changes of the program that produce the desired end re-sult. Lots of work produces multiple outcomes over time, which equals impact. Your impact is the answer to the question: What does success look like?

Example: Students will develop stronger studying skills, and parents will be more active in students' education and in the school.

Outcomes: The short-term change that an initiative or program produces; the in-tended result within a one-year timeframe. The change can be in behavior, prac-tices, attitudes, or conditions. Achievement of outcomes contributes to long-term impact. "Did the program participants experience the benefits or changes intended? What evidence do we have?"

Example: As a result of the parent leadership training, all twenty parents vol-unteered five hours each a week in their child's classroom.

Outputs: The products or program activities that occur as part of your work. Out-puts might include a new brochure, the number of performances produced, and the number of people graduating from a leadership-training program. "What did we develop or create this year?"

Example: The program created a new brochure to attract parents to its train-ing, and it also piloted a new curriculum.

Results: What was achieved. Some people use *results* and *outcomes* interchangeably.

WHAT IS A LOGIC MODEL?

A logic model is an approach to planning and evaluation that "maps" the ultimate results you seek to achieve and the steps that must be followed to achieve those results.

A logic model asks you to identify specifics for each of the following five areas:

1. *Inputs* (resources needed to support a program)
2. *Strategies* (the activities and services you are using to reach your goal)
3. *Outputs* (what you produce—a newsletter, a lobby day in the state capital)
4. *Outcomes* (the broader result of the output: spoke with seven legislators about our position; informed three hundred community residents about lead poisoning)
5. *Impact* (aggregate or ultimate effect of a sustained program—new legislation; reduced lead poisoning in children by 10 percent)

Types of Evaluation

The term *rolling evaluation* is one the authors use to describe an evaluation process wherein smaller organizations choose one or two questions or areas per year to evaluate and build evaluation learning year-by-year, over time. Other types of evaluation are as follows:

External	Conducted by someone who is not on the project or program staff
Formative	An examination of a program or project in process
Impact	Gauges the extent to which a program causes change toward the desired ends
Internal	Characterized by the use of internal staff or of contractors closely bound to an organization to conduct evaluation activity
Outcome	Gauges the extent to which a program causes change toward the desired ends, using outcome measurement
Participatory	Includes clients or beneficiaries in the process
Process	Focuses on the quality of program components or implementation
Summative	Conducted at (or toward) the end of a program or project

Sample Completed Evaluation Planning Worksheet

Evaluation Planning Worksheet

Organization Name: East Morgan Neighborhood Network

Date: January 4, 2005

SUMMARY

Evaluation Goal for FY05–06:
The evaluation goal for this year is to determine the accomplishments and challenges of implementing the Health Career Campaign last year. We realize that we had unexpected challenges that surprised us.

The questions we will ask to learn what we want to know are:

1. One year into the hotline, what goals and/or expectations have been met/not met? What did you hope would happen that has—and that hasn't?

2. How should priorities be changed to put more focus on achieving the goals?

Evaluation Planning Worksheet, Cont'd

WHAT WE'RE EVALUATING

Check the box that applies:

The evaluation goal indicated above means we are evaluating

- ☐ A PRIORITY, or priority area, or an aspect of our mission as a whole
- ☐ A piece of our ORGANIZATION, one of the structures that enable our work
- ☑ A particular PROGRAM
- ☐ An aspect of a program, a STRATEGY within a program area
- ☐ A specific GRANT

TIMING AND BACKGROUND

The block of time we'll look at is from: January 1, 2004, to December 31, 2005.

We will evaluate the activity that takes place in this area during that period of time.

DESCRIPTION/Brief history of program or area to be evaluated

The Health Career Awareness Campaign (the Campaign) is designed to inform East Morgan residents about the variety of interesting and well-paying careers in health care and create interest among residents in pursuing a new career in health care (either a first-time employment opportunity at an entry-level position or a higher-level position within a current field).

METHODS/How we'll gather information to answer our questions

To answer Evaluation Question 1 (What goals and/or expectations have been met/not met? What did you hope would happen that has—and that hasn't?) we will measure the following:

Evaluation Planning Worksheet, Cont'd

Measure 1: Number of residents who called, based on outreach efforts, and the result of the calls

Measure 2: Whether we met our budget, timetable, and stated service goals

We will measure this using the following techniques (check all that apply):

- ☑ Record review:
- ☐ Observation of:
- ☑ Interviews of staff and committee members:
- ☐ Focus groups with:
- ☐ Surveys of:

To answer Evaluation Question 2 (How should priorities be changed to put more focus on achieving the goals?) we will measure the following:

Measure 1: Stakeholder/partner perceptions of the Campaign and its assumptions

Measure 2: Number of partners interested in this effort

We will measure this using the following techniques (check all that apply):

- ☑ Record review: internal records and other program models
- ☐ Observation of:
- ☑ Interviews of: staff, funders, training program providers, health care employers, and workforce policymakers and practitioners
- ☐ Focus groups with:
- ☐ Surveys of:

Evaluation Planning Worksheet, Cont'd

USES/DISSEMINATION/AUDIENCE FOR THE EVALUATION

Once completed, we will share the results of this evaluation with:

✓ Board and staff

✓ Funder(s): Jane Smith Foundation

___ Other: _____

    We will use it to:

✓ Plan for next year _____

✓ Other: Train Staff

STAFF/CONSULTANT RESPONSIBILITIES

Sam Smith, executive director, will be responsible for the management and oversight of all evaluation activities, including convening staff and board teams to review plans, progress, findings, and implication.

Amy Jones, program manager, will be responsible for data collection.

The evaluation committee of the board will be responsible for data analysis and reporting.

The evaluation committee and the executive director will review and edit the final report.

BOARD RESPONSIBILITIES

The liaison or board committee for evaluation consists of:
Tom Klunk, Patty Santos, Mary Merth

The final report will be completed by June 2006.

We have allocated $2,500 toward the anticipated costs of this evaluation, which include mailings for surveys, food for meetings, and fees.

Sample Evaluation Report Outline

You understand why it's necessary to do an evaluation, and you have a sense of the basic steps you'll be following. But what does an evaluation look like, in the end?

In order to help your board and staff understand from the beginning where you're headed with the evaluation process, we offer you a quick picture of where you'll end up. Part of the confusion around evaluation often relates to a lack of information about what the final product is supposed to be—or what it should look like in the end. To help your board and staff come to a shared understanding of what style or format best fits your organization, you might begin by calling colleagues and asking for copies of any evaluation documents they've done in the past few years. As you'll see, there is room for many different approaches, but in one way or another, most evaluation work results in a document containing the following elements:

FINAL REPORT

Evaluation of (Area)

Purpose of the Evaluation: overall evaluation goals (why the evaluation was conducted and its intended use; what questions are being addressed by the evaluation)

Organization description and brief history

Description of program being evaluated

Methodology

Types of information that were collected

How information was collected

How information was analyzed

Learnings (bullet-point findings from your analysis of the information)

Recommendations for using the information (regarding the specific alterations that should now be made relative to the program)

Appendixes might include

Instruments used to collect data or information

Data, such as charts, tables, survey responses

Testimonials, comments made by stakeholders of the program

Case studies of users of the program

Any related literature

Program Evaluation Standards

The following program evaluation standards were developed by the Joint Committee on Standards for Educational Evaluation (AJCSEE) and have been adopted by numerous professional associations. These standards can be used as a guide for designing, managing, and assessing the evaluation process.

UTILITY STANDARDS

The utility standards are intended to ensure that an evaluation will serve the information needs of intended users.

U1 Stakeholder Identification: Persons involved in or affected by the evaluation should be identified, so that their needs can be addressed.

U2 Evaluator Credibility: The persons conducting the evaluation should be both trustworthy and competent to perform the evaluation, so that the evaluation findings achieve maximum credibility and acceptance.

U3 Information Scope and Selection: Information collected should be broadly selected to address pertinent questions about the program and be responsive to the needs and interests of clients and other specified stakeholders.

U4 Values Identification: The perspectives, procedures, and rationale used to interpret the findings should be carefully described, so that the bases for value judgments are clear.

U5 Report Clarity: Evaluation reports should clearly describe the program being evaluated, including its context, and the purposes, procedures, and findings of the evaluation, so that essential information is provided and easily understood.

U6 Report Timeliness and Dissemination: Significant interim findings and evaluation reports should be disseminated to intended users, so that they can be used in a timely fashion.

U7 Evaluation Impact: Evaluations should be planned, conducted, and reported in ways that encourage follow-through by stakeholders, so that the likelihood that the evaluation will be used is increased.

FEASIBILITY STANDARDS

The feasibility standards are intended to ensure that an evaluation will be realistic, prudent, diplomatic, and frugal.

F1 Practical Procedures: The evaluation procedures should be practical, to keep disruption to a minimum while needed information is obtained.

F2 Political Viability: The evaluation should be planned and conducted with anticipation of the different positions of various interest groups, so that their cooperation may be obtained, and so that possible attempts by any of these groups to curtail evaluation operations or to bias or misapply the results can be averted or counteracted.

F3 Cost-Effectiveness: The evaluation should be efficient and produce information of sufficient value, so that the resources expended can be justified.

PROPRIETY STANDARDS

The propriety standards are intended to ensure that an evaluation will be conducted legally, ethically, and with due regard for the welfare of those involved in the evaluation, as well as those affected by its results.

P1 Service Orientation: Evaluations should be designed to assist organizations to address and effectively serve the needs of the full range of targeted participants.

P2 Formal Agreements: Obligations of the formal parties to an evaluation (what is to be done, how, by whom, when) should be agreed to in writing, so that these parties are obligated to adhere to all conditions of the agreement or formally to renegotiate it.

P3 Rights of Human Subjects: Evaluations should be designed and conducted to respect and protect the rights and welfare of human subjects.

P4 Human Interactions: Evaluators should respect human dignity and worth in their interactions with other persons associated with an evaluation, so that participants are not threatened or harmed.

P5 Complete and Fair Assessment: The evaluation should be complete and fair in its examination and recording of strengths and weaknesses of the program being evaluated, so that strengths can be built upon and problem areas addressed.

P6 Disclosure of Findings: The formal parties to an evaluation should ensure that the full set of evaluation findings along with pertinent limitations are made accessible to the persons affected by the evaluation and any others with express legal rights to receive the results.

P7 Conflict of Interest: Conflict of interest should be dealt with openly and honestly, so that it does not compromise the evaluation processes and results.

P8 Fiscal Responsibility: The evaluator's allocation and expenditure of resources should reflect sound accountability procedures and otherwise be prudent and ethically responsible, so that expenditures are accounted for and appropriate.

ACCURACY STANDARDS

The accuracy standards are intended to ensure that an evaluation will reveal and convey technically adequate information about the features that determine worth or merit of the program being evaluated.

A1 Program Documentation: The program being evaluated should be described and documented clearly and accurately, so that the program is clearly identified.

A2 Context Analysis: The context in which the program exists should be examined in enough detail, so that its likely influences on the program can be identified.

A3 Described Purposes and Procedures: The purposes and procedures of the evaluation should be monitored and described in enough detail, so that they can be identified and assessed.

A4 Defensible Information Sources: The sources of information used in a program evaluation should be described in enough detail, so that the adequacy of the information can be assessed.

A5 Valid Information: The information-gathering procedures should be chosen or developed and then implemented so that they will assure that the interpretation arrived at is valid for the intended use.

A6 Reliable Information: The information-gathering procedures should be chosen or developed and then implemented so that they will assure that the information obtained is sufficiently reliable for the intended use.

A7 Systematic Information: The information collected, processed, and reported in an evaluation should be systematically reviewed, and any errors found should be corrected.

A8 Analysis of Quantitative Information: Quantitative information in an evaluation should be appropriately and systematically analyzed so that evaluation questions are effectively answered.

A9 Analysis of Qualitative Information: Qualitative information in an evaluation should be appropriately and systematically analyzed so that evaluation questions are effectively answered.

A10 Justified Conclusions: The conclusions reached in an evaluation should be explicitly justified, so that stakeholders can assess them.

A11 Impartial Reporting: Reporting procedures should guard against distortion caused by personal feelings and biases of any party to the evaluation, so that evaluation reports fairly reflect the evaluation findings.

A12 Metaevaluation: The evaluation itself should be formatively and summatively evaluated against these and other pertinent standards, so that its conduct is appropriately guided, and, on completion, stakeholders can closely examine its strengths and weaknesses.

ACKNOWLEDGMENTS

The experiences of many colleagues helped shape this book. We are grateful for the advice, contributions, and support of many people, especially Kim Klein, who launched this project and whose perspective guided it.

We want to thank the following individuals for their input and generosity: Jill Baldwin, Marjorie Craig Benton, Betsy Brill, Kassie Davis, Jackie Kaplan, Jeanne Kracher, Valerie Lies and the staff of The Donors Forum of Chicago, Marcia Lipetz, Pat Logue, Jo Moore, Susie Quern Pratt, Ruth Barrett Rendler, Janice Rodgers, Ken Rolling, Lloyd Sachs, Unmi Song, Dimitra Tasiouras, and Kris Torkelson.

We appreciate the thorough, thoughtful, and supportive editorial team at Jossey-Bass: Dorothy Hearst, Allison Brunner, and Jesse Wiley.

Last, for the example they set and the enormous contribution they make, we want to acknowledge some of the many nonprofit organizations that we have learned from, organizations doing their level best every day: America's Second Harvest, Amnesty International USA, Chicago Foundation for Women, Chicago Global Donors Network, Chicago Jobs Council, Girls Best Friend Foundation, Illinois Caucus on Adolescent Health, Lambda Legal Defense and Education Fund, Parents for Public Schools, The Peace Museum, Project Exploration, North Lawndale Employment Network, Rock for Reading, and Working Together in the Schools.

ABOUT THE AUTHORS

Marcia Festen and *Marianne Philbin* are consultants with extensive experience working with nonprofit organizations on issues related to evaluation and planning, capacity building, and organizational development. In addition to *Level Best,* they are coauthors of *How Effective Nonprofits Work: A Guide for Donors, Board Members and Foundation Officers* (Forum of Regional Associations of Grantmakers, 2002).

Marcia Festen is an independent consultant to a broad range of foundations and nonprofit organizations. Her consulting practice focuses on program development and evaluation. Prior to starting her consulting practice, Festen was a senior program officer at the John D. and Catherine T. MacArthur Foundation. While at the Foundation, she designed, implemented, and evaluated grantmaking strategies in the areas of youth and community development, women's health, and access to economic opportunity. She has also worked as a case manager for Project Match—a welfare-to-work demonstration program in the Cabrini Green public housing development in Chicago, Illinois.

Festen is coauthor of *A Funder's Guide to Using A Gender Lens* (Chicago Women in Philanthropy, 2000), *A Funder's Guide to Youth Development Programs* (Donors Forum of Chicago, 1998), and *Leveraging New Funds to Support Human Rights Organizations* (International Human Rights Funders' Group, 2001).

Marianne Philbin has more than twenty-five years of experience in the nonprofit sector. In addition to her work with foundation and nonprofit clients, she is an instructor on grantmaking, evaluation, and nonprofit governance for The Donors Forum of Chicago and is a lecturer at Northwestern University's School of Continuing Studies.

Philbin served as development director for the Chicago Annenberg Challenge, executive director of The Chicago Foundation for Women, and executive director of The Peace Museum. She has played leadership roles on numerous nonprofit boards, ranging from Amnesty International USA to Project Exploration. She is coauthor of *How to Do a Lot with a Lot: A Guide to Community Gardening* (Neighbor Space, 2006), contributor to *Women, Philanthropy and Social Change: Visions for a Just Society* (Tufts University Press, 2005), *The Grassroots Fundraising Journal* (Chardon Press), and numerous other publications.

REFERENCES

Abravanel, M. *Surveying Clients About Outcomes,* Urban Institute Series on Outcome Management for Nonprofits. Washington, D.C.: Urban Institute, 2003. Available online: www.urban.org/url.cfm?ID=310840. Access date: May 14, 2006.

Atkinson, C., and Philbin, M. *How to Do a Lot With a Lot: A Guide to Community Gardening.* Chicago: Neighbor Space, 2006.

Bothwell, R. *Foundation Funding of Grassroots Organizations.* Washington D.C.: National Committee for Responsive Philanthropy, 2000.

Brinkerhoff, R. *The Success Case Method: Find Out Quickly What's Working and What's Not.* San Francisco: Berrett-Koehler, 2003.

Capek, M. E. *Nonprofit/Philanthropic Sector Scan.* Newark N.J.: Center for Nonprofit and Philanthropic Leadership, Rutgers University Business School, 2004.

Checkoway, B., and Richards-Schuster, K. *Participatory Evaluation with Young People.* Ann Arbor: Program for Youth and Community, School of Social Work, University of Michigan, 2005.

Crossroads Fund Grantee Progress Report: Questions for Evaluating, Gauging Impact and Measuring Effectiveness of Your Work. Chicago: Crossroads Fund, 2006.

Festen, M., and Philbin, M. *How Effective Nonprofits Work: A Guide for Donors, Board Members and Foundation Staff.* Washington, D.C.: Forum of Regional Association of Grantmakers, 2002.

Ganz, M. "What Is Organizing?" Paper for the course "Organizing: People, Power and Change," Kennedy School of Government, Harvard University, 1996.

Grantee Annual Follow-Up Report. Chicago: Polk Bros. Foundation, 2006.

Gray, S. T., and Stockdill, S. H. "Evaluation With Power." Washington D.C.: Independent Sector, 1995.

Heartland Alliance. Mission statement, 2005. Available online: www.heartlandalliance.org.

Joint Committee on Standards, "Program Evaluation Standards," (2nd ed.). Thousand Oaks, Calif.: Sage, 1994.

McNamara, C. "Overview of Methods to Collect Information." Minneapolis: Authenticity Counsulting LLC, 1998.

Puntenney, D. *Measuring Social Change Investments.* San Francisco: Women's Funding Network, 2002.

Quern Pratt, S. *Putting Evaluation to Work for You.* PowerPoint presentation for Donors Forum of Chicago members. Chicago. Undated.

Sanders, J. R. *The Program Evaluation Standards: How to Assess Evaluations of Educational Programs.* Thousand Oaks, Calif.: Sage, 1994.

Urban Institute. *Surveying Clients About Outcomes.* Washington, D.C.: Urban Institute, 2003.

W. K. Kellogg Foundation Logic Model Development Guide. Battlecreek, Mich.: W. K. Kellogg Foundation, 2004.

Women's Funding Network, San Francisco. "Making the Case: An Interactive Online Tool for Measuring Social Change." Available online: www.info@wfnet.org.

York, P. *Learning As We Go: Making Evaluation Work for Everyone.* A briefing paper for funders and nonprofits. New York: TCC Group, 2003.

Zimmerman, R. *Measuring Success and Making Change with Evaluation.* Minneapolis: Minnesota Council of Nonprofits, 2004.

INDEX

Dissemination planning, 101–102
Documentation review, 76, 78

E

East Morgan Neighborhood Network, 15, 77, 99

Evaluation: "The Big Question" to ask during, 59; clear goals to guide, 45–46, 51–54; conducting an in-house, 35; conducting research versus, 6–7; creating effective organizations with, 8–9; flow of nonprofit work and nature of, 14; golden rule of, 94, 106; grant reports versus, 44; *if-then* statement on assumptions of, 55, 57–58, 77, 80; less and more effective nonprofits and, 33; of potential risks or rewards of, 9; public opinion as, 4; rolling, 23–26, 27, 69; using contractual help for, 34–35; the wrong reasons for conducting, 8. *See also* Outcome evaluation; Process evaluation

Evaluation definitions: jargon, 14; as planning not judging, 5–6; reframed as power instead of pain, 3–5; supporting steps for understanding, 10; traditional test connotation of, 3

Evaluation framework: basic common-sense evaluation tasks, 13–14, 16–17; characteristics of less or more effective, 16–17; on how to get started, 20, 22–23; logic models, 14, 68; on rolling evaluation method, 23–26, 27; standards considerations, 20, 96; supporting steps for the basic, 26; on what to evaluate, 18–20

Evaluation jargon, 14

Evaluation Learning Continuum, 36–37

Evaluation planning: described, 13; Evaluation Planning Worksheet, 40–43; evaluations feeding directly into next, 97, 102; fitting funders' needs into, 44–45; how you can prepare for, 46–47; impact on what you learn, 35–37; less and more effective approaches to, 16; less and more effective nonprofits and, 33; Meeting Agenda 3 for, 49–50; as part of strategic planning, 102, 103–105; quick review of organizational readiness, 29–30; step-by-step, 38–43; supporting steps for, 48–49. *See also* Strategic planning

Evaluation planning steps: 1: conducting board and staff orientation, 38; 2: determining roles and job responsibilities, 38; 3: identifying what you are already doing, 38; 4: developing a time frame, 38–39; 5: developing evaluation budget, 39; 6: clarifying overarching goals for programs or initiatives, 39; 7: zeroing in on questions you want to explore, 39; 8: committing the plan to paper, 39–43

Evaluation Planning Worksheet, 40–43

Evaluation preparation: Meeting Agenda 1 for, 11; Meeting Agenda 2 for, 27

Evaluation results: challenging or disappointing, 98, 100–101; dissemination of, 101–102; feeding results into cycle of planning, 97, 102; how not to use, 98; how to use, 97; making the case for supporting, 99; Meeting Agenda 6 on learning and using, 107; problems associated with, 100–101; when and where to use, 98. *See also* Outcomes; Using task

Evaluation roles, 38

Evaluation strategies: building on simple and logical, 22; rolling evaluation method as, 23–26, 27, 69

Exercises: determining top priorities of evaluation, 19; evaluation fears and misperceptions, 7; What's Your Theory of Change?, 56. *See also* Worksheets

F

Fears of evaluation, 7

Festen, M., 33

Financial management, 32. *See also* Budgets

Focus groups: data-collection using, 76, 78; developing questions for, 84–87

Formative evaluation, 14

Funders: fitting their needs into evaluation planning, 44–45; interviews taken from, 93; progress reports to, 47; questions to anticipate evaluation concerns of, 47–48; sharing evaluation results with, 101–102; year-end grant reports to, 44. *See also* Stakeholders

G

Ganz, M., 68

Goals: assessing achievement of objectives or, 61; clarifying program or initiative overarching, 39; evaluation guidance through clear, 45–46, 51–55; Meeting Agenda 3 on evaluation, 49–50. *See also* Outcomes

The Golden Rule of Evaluation, 94, 106

Governance, 31

Grassroots organizations: evaluation questions asked by, 64–67; how to be answerable in context of, 67–68; ideas for measuring organizing efforts for, 69. *See also* Social change

Gray, S. T., 18

H

Heartland Alliance, 50

I

If-then statement: goal statement determining information tracking, 77, 80; including basic evaluation assumptions, 55, 57–58

In-house evaluations, 35

Information: drawing conclusions from, 92–97; the golden rule of evaluation on, 94; making use of your, 91–92; Meeting Agenda 6 learning and using results of, 107; organizing your, 92; tracking, 73–89; using what you learn from, 97–98; ways to analyze survey, 96

Initiative goals, 39

Instinctual nonprofit operations, 1–2

Interviews: data-collection using, 76, 78; developing questions for, 84–87, 93; sample summary of, 93

J

Job responsibilities, 38

L

Learning: described, 14; determining what you want to learn, 21; evaluation continuum of, 36–37; how planning affects, 35–37; less and more effective approaches to, 17; Meeting Agenda 6 on using results of evaluation, 107; using evaluation, 97–98

Lipetz, M., 9

Logic models: definition of, 14; W.K. Kellogg Foundation Logic Model Development Guide on, 68

M

"Making the Case," 67

McLuhan, M., 60

McNamara, C., 79

Meeting agendas: 1: preparing for evaluation, 11; 2: preparing for evaluation, 27; 3: focusing our mission and evaluation priorities, 49–50; 4: determining evaluation questions, 70–71;

determining evaluation questions on, 22–23; determining what we want to learn about, 21; less and more effective nonprofits and, 31; questions assessing outcomes of, 61–62. *See also* Nonprofits

Public opinion evaluation, 4

Puntenney, D. L., 64

Q

Questionnaires, 78

Questions: to ask what you really want to know, 64; "The Big Question," 59; community gardening, 86–87; comparisons of responses from same or multiple, 96; Democracy Begins Here and sample, 65; determining the right, 59–64; developing SMART, 68; developing survey, focus group, and interview, 84–87, 93; focusing in on evaluation, 39; guidelines on wording, 85; if or then, 57–58; Meeting Agenda 4 determining evaluation, 70–71; for outcome and process evaluations, 55; rolling evaluation use of, 23, 24–25; supporting steps for asking the right, 69. *See also* The right questions

R

Resource development, 32

Results. *See* Evaluation results

Richards-Schuster, K., 75

The right questions: for better understanding your outcomes, 61–62; improving the delivery of your message, 60–61; reflecting on and improving your "product," 59–60; for sustaining your organizations, 62–64. *See also* Questions

Rolling evaluation method: advantages of using, 23–24, 26; described, 23; Meet-ing Agenda 2 on, 27; questions used as part of, 23, 24–25

S

Sanders, J., 89

SMART evaluation questions, 68

Social change: advocacy organizations evaluation of impact on, 64–67; capturing the benefits of progress toward, 67–68; five indicators of, 67; ideas for measuring organizing efforts for, 69; slow process of large-scale, 64; Theory of Change and, 55–56. *See also* Advocacy organizations; Grassroots organizations; Nonprofit work

Song, U., 9

Staff: conducting planning orientation for, 38; strategic planning involving volunteer, 104–105

Stakeholders: community as, 93, 95; comparisons across subgroups of, 96; decisions regarding what data to use from, 76–77; sharing evaluation results with, 101–102; strategic planning involving, 104–105. *See also* Funders

Standards: comparison against best practices and, 96; considering field or discipline, 20

Starting evaluation, 20, 22–23

Stockdill, S. H., 18

Strategic planning: incorporating evaluation into process of, 103–104; involving volunteer leadership, 104–105; tying evaluation planning into, 102, 103. *See also* Evaluation planning

Structure (nonprofits), 31

Summative evaluation, 14

Surveys: comparing data from previous, 96; data-collection using, 76, 78;

Made in the USA
San Bernardino, CA
06 December 2013